# PARENTING A
# VIOLENT
# CHILD

There are those who think that problems are solved through effort. These people merrily succeed in keeping themselves and others busy. Problems are only solved through awareness. In fact – where there is awareness – problems do not arise.

Anthony De Mello, *Awakenings*

# PARENTING A VIOLENT CHILD

## Steps to taking back control and creating a happier home

## ISLAY DOWNEY
## and KIM FURNISH

**Illustrations by Amy Michelle Downey**

DARTON·LONGMAN+TODD

*To all the parents who have generously shared
their stories with us and to our own parents
whose stories shaped our lives.*

First published in 2015 by
Darton, Longman and Todd Ltd
1 Spencer Court
140 – 142 Wandsworth High Street
London   SW18 4JJ

ISBN 978-0-232-53147-3

A catalogue record for this book is available from the British Library

Designed and produced by Judy Linard

Printed and bound in Great Britain by Bell & Bain, Glasgow

# CONTENTS

The chance for change comes when you put down the magnifying glass and pick up the mirror.

# INTRODUCTION

This book has come about because of the hidden nature of child to parent violence. We, Islay and Kim, have experience of working with parents and families in a variety of settings. Throughout our combined 25 years of working with families the issue of child to parent violence has come up time and time again. Many parents feel ashamed to talk openly about the problem and feel blamed for how their child is behaving. This then keeps it hidden. This book has been written to encourage parents who may be feeling powerless; it will help you look at ways to take back the control in a loving way and enjoy your family again.

The information in this book has been gained by facilitating hundreds of groups and workshops where parents have been generous in sharing with us their struggles. The insights and strategies gained from attending the groups have been successful in reducing violence in families.

Many parents think that by going to a parenting group they will be judged as a bad parent. It is well worth taking that risk. Going to a parenting group means that you have recognised that things need to improve for you and your child. We strongly recommend that you consider taking this step to support any changes in your parenting relationship. If you are unable to do so then we hope that you are able to use this book as the next best thing: a parenting group in a book.

You may be thinking that your child needs to change; change is hard but it is necessary if you want to break established patterns of behaviour. We are going to encourage *you* to take the first steps towards change and ask *you* to take responsibility for *your* own behaviour. It is quite easy to pick up a magnifying glass and identify the problems that your child brings to your life. What we will be asking you to do is to pick up a mirror, look into it and see how your behaviour is contributing to the situation.

We will be following six parents, as they explore what is within their power to change and what is not. We will look at how they deal with the situations that they face in their family life. We will encourage you, the reader, to make links to your own situation which will give you the confidence to make changes. The parents in the book are not real; however their stories are.

Throughout the book the six parents will be asking for help with violent episodes such as:

- Angry words
- Kicking off/tantrums
- Trashing the house or their room
- Physical attacks
- Verbal abuse.

By showing how this would be discussed in a parenting group our aim is to help you understand your own behaviour and your child's behaviour. The message from this book is that there is hope. Hope brings opportunity for growth and new patterns of behaviour, which can lead to:

- Fewer arguments
- More respect
- Taking back control
- Living in a happier home.

Managing violent behaviour is exhausting and draining. It can leave you feeling lost and confused. Our experience of working with families suggests that these things can help:

- Having a positive attitude
- Being confident in your abilities

# INTRODUCTION

- Recognising your progress
- Using a support system.

As you journey through the book we will encourage and support you towards these qualities. In each chapter there will be:

BEHAVIOUR TIPS

NURTURE TIPS

for you

your child

*and* REFLECTIONS

The nurture tips have been designed to create a nurturing relationship between your child and yourself.

The behaviour tips will guide you towards teaching your child appropriate behaviour.

The reflection points at the end of each chapter are an opportunity to pause and apply the learning to your own situation.

# 1

# IN THE ZONE

 **Look for the positive.** Even the most challenging child will be doing something right. Start to notice the positive behaviour.

The parents have arrived at the group and they appear nervous. They sit in the room not talking to each other and the atmosphere is tense. Some of the parents still have their coats on despite it being very warm. Their arms are folded tightly, as if they are protecting themselves from what is about to happen. Some of them stare straight ahead and others look at the floor. They are concerned about what they are going to be asked to do and say. They each feel that they are the only one going through the worst possible situation; how could anyone else possibly know what they are going through. Islay asks them to chat to someone they don't know and to find out three things that they have in common. The room takes on a different vibe. Everyone starts to feel more relaxed as they realise that maybe they're not so different after all. As they listen to what is being said, the parents learn who will be sharing their journey:

**Margaret, single mum of Damien (12).**

**Anne and Darren, parents of Mikki (8). Anne has 3 older children, Sophie, Thomas and Peter. Peter lives with them.**

**Martin, single dad of four children: John (12), Jessie (8), Lucy (5), Kyle (3).**

**Paris, single mum of Riley (16).**

**Angie, mum of Harry (9).**

Islay: *There are many reasons why children can become violent either physically or verbally. Sadly it appears to becoming more common. Violent behaviour breeds in secrecy, and can control and isolate you to the point that you feel like you are the only one going through this. However hard it is, it is important to talk about it as this will be the first stage of changing the situation. It is about acknowledging the reality of what is happening today.*

The parents start to open up and question why their child is violent:

Anne: *Why is Mikki so angry? I've been good to her, we haven't hit her so why is she so aggressive?*

Margaret: *How can Damien be hitting me when I only want what's best for him?*

Some of the parents justify their child's behaviour:

Angie: *I suppose it's good that he's hitting me and not someone else.*

Martin: *It happens whenever he doesn't get what he wants, or if I try to say no to him.*

Islay: *Regardless of why it's happening, experiencing violent behaviour from your child may be accompanied by feelings of shame, guilt, and loss of control.*

The parents respond by sharing similar feelings:

Darren: *It's so shameful – how can I tell someone that I can't control my child? I feel so frustrated. There must be something wrong with her.*

Paris: *Everyone else seems to have such perfect children.*

Islay: *You have all taken the first step by asking for help. The challenge for you all now is to not take things personally. You have the opportunity to change things if you recognise the power you hold and you are able to ditch the feelings of guilt and blame.*

 **Stay calm.** Think of some ways to stay calm. It might be walking away from a situation, it might be taking some deep breaths; do whatever works for you.

Kim draws this diagram on the flip chart:

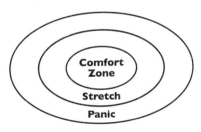

Kim: *Let's look at how we feel and what happens to us when we attempt to make changes in our behaviour. I want to talk you through the three zones that we operate in:*

- Comfort Zone – the familiar
- Stretch Zone – the challenge
- Panic Zone – the step too far

(Karl Rohnke)

The parents are asked what being in their comfort zone means to them.

Angie: *I think it is where I feel safe, secure and happy.*

Martin: *For me it is about being respected, feeling comfortable and in control.*

Kim: *In your comfort zone you will feel any or all of those things but what about if I asked you what is familiar to you?*

The parents' faces change and so do their words.

Margaret: *What's familiar for me is arguments; that's all we do at home.*

Anne: *I would like to feel safe and secure but mostly I feel miserable and unhappy.*

Martin: *There is no peace in our house; it's chaos most of the time.*

The parents agree that their day-to-day life is less like the comfort zone they desire and more like the chaos others have described.

**Stop shouting.** Start to recognise when you are shouting, stop then listen.

Kim: *The next zone is the stretch zone, what does it feel like when you are in your stretch zone? Some of you may have gone into your stretch zone by coming to the group.*

Anne: *I was really nervous, I didn't know what to expect.*

Margaret: *Getting here was hard. I was apprehensive. I didn't know who was going to be here or what we would do.*

Paris: *I couldn't wait to get here. I am hopeful, excited — I want things to change.*

Kim: *What was going on in your body? How did that feel?*

Anne: *I could feel my heart racing.*

Margaret: *My mouth was dry, when someone asked me a question I couldn't speak properly.*

Kim: When we step out of our comfort zone we all experience those physical sensations and it can feel really uncomfortable. The stretch zone is where we learn. If we feel too uncomfortable we can quickly try to get back into our comfort/familiar zone. The only way to learn is to stay with these feelings.

Islay: When I am asked a maths question my mind goes blank and I think I don't know the answer. Experience has taught me that if I stay with the uncomfortable feeling I may well come up with the right answer. I have had to get over the temptation to say immediately 'I don't know the answer' to avoid discomfort.

The parents recognised that they had stretched themselves by coming to the group. They had experienced the uncomfortable feelings and stayed with them. Now they had become more comfortable and were more relaxed.

Kim: *Has there been a time when your child did something that you wanted them to do, something that they wouldn't normally do?*

The parents appear confused but then Paris remembers something that happened recently.

Paris: *Riley got up and went to school, I couldn't believe that! I didn't do anything differently, he just went and he came back quite cheerfully. He never goes to school without kicking off.*

Kim: *How did you respond to that?*

Paris: *It worried me. I thought this is not going to last. I told him that too, which then caused an argument.*

Kim: *When things start to go the way we want them to, like Riley going to school without a fuss, we can go into the stretch zone. Sometimes we are so used to a familiar behaviour that it seems strange when it changes. Without realising what is going on we sabotage things, we stop them from changing. We need to get better at recognising what we, as parents, are doing to keep the situation stuck.*

Islay: *What might it feel like if we enter the panic zone, the 'step too far'?*

Angie: *When you can't breathe or even think straight.*

Margaret: *I hate that feeling, I go all hot and get upset.*

Martin: *Is that like panic attacks?*

Islay: *Yes, panic attacks are very common. It puts our body under a lot of strain to stay in panic for too long so it's vital that we find ways to cope with it.*

Anne: *I had a panic attack once; I really thought it was the end of me, it felt like I was going to die. My friend calmed me down and got me to do some deep breathing. I felt a bit stupid afterwards. I don't know why it happened.*

Kim: *What does anyone here do to help themselves stay out of panic?*

Anne: *Walking away has helped me. It stops me reacting to Mikki. I used to get so angry that I would say awful things to Mikki. I wish Darren could just walk away.*

Darren gives Anne an odd look,

Darren: *She really winds me up, but I'm not that bad.*

Kim: *We are going to try different strategies throughout the sessions to stay out of the panic zone and keep in the stretch zone. Anything that you can do to stay calm and relaxed will help you to make some changes to behaviour.*

Islay: *This week start to notice whether you are in the comfort, stretch or panic zone and what the triggers have been for you. This will give you useful information about your behaviour and your child's behaviour.*

As the parents get ready to leave the group they are already beginning to take on board some of the things that have been talked about in the session. Martin is hopeful that the sessions may stop some of the shouting and arguments in his family. He is doubtful though that anything can be done about the overcrowding in his house. Not only that but John has recently been diagnosed with ADHD and Jessie is showing very similar behaviour. It will only be a matter of time before Lucy and Kyle are going to end up behaving in the same way. Martin recognises that he doesn't handle things very well and people tell him that he should accept the help he is offered but mostly he feels judged about his ability as a parent.

Angie is looking very unhappy. She doesn't feel like she fits in the group. She is married and they are very comfortably off. Harry goes to private school and is a bright child. However many of the feelings other parents describe she recognises as her own. Angie is so confused about Harry's violence towards her; he can be so nasty and is very threatening. She would have liked some answers today but it has been hard for her to speak up in the group. Angie has thought about why Harry is violent; people tell her she is too soft. As she leaves the room Angie doesn't know whether she will come back again.

 **How often do you do something relaxing for yourself?**

 # FOR REFLECTION

1. What is it like for you in your:
   - Comfort Zone – the familiar
   - Stretch Zone – the challenge
   - Panic Zone – the step too far

2. What have you learned in this chapter that will help you to behave differently when your child is being violent?

# 2
# OPPORTUNITY KNOCKS

 **Do something unexpected.** Write a positive message to your child. Leave a handwritten note on their pillow, in their lunch box – anywhere where they will find it.

Kim and Islay wondered how many of the parents would return to this session of the parenting group. They had contacted the parents during the week to find out how they were getting on at home. Angie sounded unsure whether the group was the right one for her; she didn't think that Harry was as difficult as the other children. All of the parents said that they were thinking more about how they were reacting to things.

One by one they arrived in the room, looking a bit more relaxed than they had been in the first session. They chatted to each other and sat drinking their tea and coffee until the session began.

To get the session started Islay asked the parents how their week had been and whether any of them would be happy to tell the group how they had got on.

Paris is happy to start the conversation off:

Paris: *Last week made me really think about what zone I am in and I realised how confusing it must have been for Riley when he got up to go to school and I still moaned at him. This week I have started to notice how anxious I get the minute I wake up and I've made a real effort to do some deep breathing before I get out of bed. Riley hasn't gone to school this week and he's been really rude if I say anything to him, but instead of reacting I have walked away. He's started to look a bit confused and then just says 'Oh, I see – you've been on that course and now you're ignoring me'. A couple of times I reacted and we ended up having a shouting match and he got right into my face and I got really frightened.*

Paris is visibly upset and Margaret is quick to offer her support. She understands how Paris is feeling.

Margaret: *That's how Damien is with me. He goes on and on until I react, and then I get frightened. Sometimes I think he enjoys it as I see him smirking. That makes me feel so sad that I start to cry and then he calls me a cry baby.*

Martin looks a bit shocked at hearing this.

Martin: *Sounds like he needs a firm hand. Although John can be really difficult he knows when I mean business and then he's the one who ends up crying. I'd never let my children see me crying. It's a sign of weakness. They need to learn to do what I say.*

This kind of conversation isn't really helping, as the tone is more judgmental than supportive. Kim picks up on what Paris has said and asks her what difference it had made doing the deep breathing and walking away.

Paris: *It took me a while to actually walk away but when I did do it I felt more in control and I felt stronger.*

Kim: *And what happened when you got sucked in and started shouting?*

Paris: *Riley made me feel so awful, I knew what he was doing but I found it hard to stop myself. In the end it went the way it always does — with him shouting and storming off. He didn't do what I'd asked him to do; he left the house and was out all night. I was so relieved when he came back that I cooked him breakfast. He apologised and then went off to bed. I ended up doing the washing up.*

---

**Take time out.** Walk away until things have calmed down and then — this is the really important part — come back and discuss it. If you find it hard to walk away because you are afraid of the escalating violence try this:

Position yourself in the middle of the room, close your eyes, put your arms straight out in front of you and say, 'I am feeling stressed, I need to do my deep breathing exercise'. Take a long deep breath in through your nose and slowly breathe out from your mouth. Do this twice, keeping your eyes closed. The chances are your child will stop what they are doing. Then open your eyes, smile at them, say, 'Thank you, I feel much better now'. Leave the room and make a cup of tea.

---

Islay: *Did anyone look to see what their child was doing right?*

They all keep quiet and then Margaret speaks up:

Margaret: *It's hard to see that with Damien. I keep finding money going from my purse. I don't know if Damien is taking it. I'm never very sure how much I have in there but recently I went to get some money out and I know I had £10 and it wasn't there. I don't want to accuse Damien because he can get so nasty.*

Angie has stayed quiet, but is listening intently.

Angie: *Hearing you talk has taken me back to when I was younger. My brother used to steal from my parents. There were always massive arguments. I hated it and I used to go upstairs to my room to get away from it. My brother ended up in prison. I'm so scared that Harry will end up like him.*

Islay: *It's such a challenge to see the positive in our children's behaviour when our experience is that they get it wrong. We end up fearing the worst and then in a strange way our fears become true. Was anyone able to see the positive and to just comment on that?*

Darren: *I felt a bit sore after Anne said last week that she wished I could walk away when Mikki starts. So this week when Mikki came home I didn't say anything to her about clearing up her mess but she put everything away anyway. Normally I'm on at Mikki to hang everything up and not leave her clothes in a heap on the floor. I was really surprised and I even managed to say thank you to her. She seemed a bit shocked and just shrugged her shoulders. I resisted the temptation to say, 'How about you do that every day'.*

Darren chuckled and looked around the room for confirmation that he had done the right thing.

Anne: *Actually you've had fewer arguments this week. I hadn't really thought about it but things have been better.*

Islay: *There are some positive steps towards change happening already. In this session we are going to look at our behaviour and try to think about why we do what we do. In our busy lives it is hard to find time to stop and think. Once we are able to stop and reflect on our behaviour we have greater choice with regards to the actions we take. We are going to look at how our behaviour can fit into four boxes as described by the Window to Self-Knowledge.*

Islay draws on the flip chart the following diagram which is based on Johari's window (Luft & Ingham, 1955).

| 1 **Shared** Things we know about ourselves and others know about us | 2 **Secret** Things we know about ourselves that others do not know |
|---|---|
| 3 **Blind** Things others know about us that we do not know | 4 **Hidden** Things neither we nor others know about us |

Islay: *The more you understand your own behaviour the bigger Box 1 becomes. This is self-awareness, it relates to how well we know and understand our own behaviour and how open we are about it. Can you think of some behaviours that would fit into this box?*

Martin: *I smoke; I know I smoke and so does anyone I'm with. I also know it's bad for me and as my non-smoking friends keep telling me so do they!*

Paris: *I have a loud voice. People keep telling me to talk quietly. They often think I'm angry when I'm not and it's because I talk loudly.*

Kim: *Yes, that's it exactly. The behaviour that belongs in Box 1 are those things that you know you do, and everyone else knows it as well.*

Islay: *Box 2 relates to the behaviours that we hide from others. Can you think what behaviour might fit within Box 2?*

They all look a bit shocked as they think they are being asked to share their secrets. But then an idea comes to Angie.

Angie: *Might that be when you buy a pair of shoes and don't tell your partner or don't tell him how much they cost?*

Laughter breaks out around the room.

Martin: *What about taking drugs or gambling?*

Angie: *Or that my child is hitting me?*

Islay: *Yes, these are our secrets and to enable Box 2 to become smaller and Box 1 to get bigger we need to be willing to share information about ourselves and open up with others. This can make us feel vulnerable; we may feel judged or criticised. With this in mind, who you confide in is very important. You will need to trust that this person has your best interests at heart. When your child is hitting you it can feel very shameful but as we've said before, actions done in secret will breed. Once you are honest about what is happening then it doesn't have the same hold over you. It's the same with something like gambling. If only one person knows, the person who is being affected by it, and they are ashamed, then the behaviour is likely to continue. Once that person is brave enough to tell others then it lifts the lid on the secrecy and it is much harder for the behaviour to continue.*

Angie: *I have felt so embarrassed by Harry's temper. I keep thinking what have I done so wrong to deserve this. I don't always tell Phillip what has happened because I know he'll just get angry and then it makes matters worse.*

Darren: *I don't always tell Anne what Mikki can be like with me. Anne's got three grown up children and they are so perfect....*

Anne: *I don't see them like that, but Mikki plays us off against each other. I do keep telling you that. We need to be honest with each other.*

Kim: *It is always hard to share what is going on but the more you are able to share the more support you can give to each other.*

Islay: *So, onto Box 3 – this is the behaviour that you don't know you do but others do. What do you think will fit in this box?*

Angie: *Someone at work told me that I roll my eyes. I was horrified as I never knew that.*

Darren: *Anne says I snore, which I'm sure I don't!*

Kim: *Yes that's right; those are great examples. The only way to get this box to be smaller is by being able to receive feedback.*

Islay: *There is a health warning here though: some feedback needs to be ignored. If you think about comments on social media sites about celebrities, some of it is ugly and not true. We have to look for the evidence when someone tells us something about ourselves to check out whether it is true or not.*

Paris: *I'm always being judged. I'll get a new friend and I'll start to confide in them – next thing I hear they've been telling my stuff to other people. I soon dump them. Something else that happens is that people put comments about me on Facebook and I get really mad. It's horrid.*

Kim: *That sounds pretty awful, Paris. Has anyone else experienced a similar situation?*

Margaret: *I don't talk to anyone. I find it hard to trust people. My experience is that most people don't care about you, they only care about themselves.*

Anne: *I have some good friends that I can trust. Sometimes they say something to me and I have to think about what they've said.*

*It's hard as I want to tell them to mind their own business. I get the school ringing me up a lot about Mikki and I used to get defensive and make excuses about her behaviour and then a friend told me that I wasn't doing her any favours by defending her all the time. Mikki used to think that she could do anything at school and I would back her up. I realised I was giving her the wrong message. It was really hard hearing that but I was grateful to my friend for pointing it out. I now check out any story Mikki gives me with the school and I usually find that Mikki has given me a distorted version of the truth.*

Paris: *Oh that has made me think. Riley would come home and tell me the teacher had shouted at him in front of all his friends and I would get so angry. I would storm up the school and demand an apology from the teacher. He'd also say that another child was picking on him and I'd have a right go at the parents in the playground. I'd then tell him that he wasn't to say anything to that child. And I'd tell the teacher.*

Kim: *It sounds like you always believed Riley's version of events.*

Paris: *Yes, I did.*

Kim: *What do you think the danger of that might be?*

Darren: *It would make them feel powerful, like they can manipulate the situation.*

Islay: *It is hard because we need to listen to our children, even their distorted version of the truth because underneath they will be telling us how they feel. However if we act on their information alone then we are putting them in charge. Can anyone think of a way of being able to listen to what they are saying and to acknowledge how they are feeling without rescuing them?*

*Anne: When Mikki comes home and says someone said something nasty to her, I say, 'That must make you sad', and then I wait for her to say either yes or no. It usually encourages her to talk about what happened and then I ask her what she might be able to do about it. We then explore together what she can do. One time she came back to me and told me that she'd talked to her friend about how hurt she was and her friend had said sorry to her; she hadn't realised that her actions had been hurtful to Mikki. Mikki has started to come and talk to me more about how she is feeling. I try not to react to her now but I get her to think for herself.*

*Paris: I'm always telling Riley what to think and feel!*

*Kim: What do you think the difference would be if you stopped telling him and just started to acknowledge?*

*Paris: He'd probably think I've gone mad but it might be worth a try.*

*Islay: Anne it sounds as if you have managed to enlarge your Box 1 by listening to your friend's advice.*

Anne looks pleased.

 **Set a good example.** If you are concerned about how much your child swears, listen to your own language and make some changes if necessary.

*Islay: We now come to Box 4, and that is our hidden self. We don't know why we do the things we do and neither does anyone else. These could be the habits that have been passed down to us or could be some instinctive reaction to something and we don't know where it has come from. We will be exploring this in more detail in the next session.*

Angie: *I've been married to my husband for 15 years and sometimes he'll react to something and when I ask why he'll say, 'I don't know why I've got so upset about it'. Is that what you mean?*

Islay: *Yes it's that exactly. It's really hard to work these things out for ourselves but the more we start to think about them the more we will start to understand ourselves. Box 4 will become smaller the more you are open to learning about yourself and you continue to explore why you behave the way you do. Sometimes your anger stems from the way you were treated as a child. You may have never considered this however it will leak out in other areas of your life. This could be through resentment, stubbornness, frustration, and a feeling of dissatisfaction with life. It's worth considering whether there are times when you are sitting in Box 4 of the Window to Self-Knowledge.*

*The Window to Self-Knowledge and the comfort, stretch, panic zones that we have previously introduced help us to understand our own behaviour. This then leads to self-awareness. Once we become more self-aware, we recognise the changes we need to make and it is possible to move from our stuck position.*

To end the session Kim asks the parents what they are taking away from Session 2.

Angie: *It's made me realise that we need to spend time as a family, having good times, otherwise all I see is what is going wrong.*

Martin: *Someone told me about geocaching and the kids love it.*

Angie: *What is geocaching? I have never heard of that.*

Martin: *It's like a worldwide treasure hunt – you can find out all about it on their website. You use your GPS on your mobile signal to get directions to the cache. It was something different and we all enjoyed it.*

Angie: *That sounds like something that we would all like to do.*

Margaret: *The comfort zone meant a lot to me. From today's session what I realise is that I am scared of moving out of my comfort zone and I really need to.*

Anne: *It's been good for me today. It has made me realise that I have already put some changes in place, but I do need to keep that going.*

Darren: *If things are going to change I need to be more honest with Anne, we need to work together not be in competition.*

Paris: *It's when you said I always believe what Riley says. I thought that was being a good mum – sticking up for my boy – but maybe I need to stop that.*

Angie: *I have enjoyed the session and I'm glad I came back. The Window to Self-Knowledge made a lot of sense to me and I am going to need some time to think about why I behave the way I do.*

Islay: *There have been some fantastic ideas and suggestions and we will look forward to hearing how you have got on in Session 3. During the next week it would be good if you could start to notice your own behaviour and the effect that has on your child.*

As the session draws to a close the parents gather their belongings and gradually leave the room. Talking in the group had made Anne see that Darren was prepared to put things right. She noticed that she was feeling more relaxed and was hopeful for a better way of life. It could be so difficult at home and she felt stuck in the middle of Darren and her older children. Sophie was so demanding and expected Anne to do exactly what she wanted. Anne wondered whether the group would help with Sophie as well as Mikki. But first of all she would focus on getting Mikki sorted by watching her own behaviour; she would keep one eye on Darren too.

Margaret was so pleased that Paris was in the group. Paris was on her own bringing up Riley just like Margaret was. Damien's dad, Richard had left them seven years ago. She hadn't really got over it yet; although Richard was violent towards her they had some good times. It ended when Richard had really got into a rage and Margaret had used all her strength to call the police. Richard had been arrested. He had left soon after that and they had not seen him since. Margaret had often thought that Damien wouldn't be like this if his dad was around.

 Eating a healthy diet is a great way to nurture yourself and is also a good example for your child.

 ## FOR REFLECTION

1. Where would you mainly put yourself in the Window of Self Knowledge? What behaviours can you identify in:
   Box 1
   Box 2

2. Has anyone ever given you any feedback about your behaviour? Did you agree with it or disagree with it?

3. What have you learnt in this chapter that will help you to behave differently when your child is being violent?

# 3

# TIMES GONE BY

 **Spend quality one-to-one time with your child.** Children thrive on small chunks of quality time. It tells your child that they are important in your life.

During the week Kim and Islay had phoned the parents to see how things were going.

One by one they all returned to the group session.

Kim: *Last week we looked at the Window to Self-Knowledge, I was wondering how you got on during the week.*

Paris: *Riley was really demanding one evening and normally I would give in just to get him away from me but this time as soon as I felt angry I tried the standing in the room idea. I didn't think I was going to be able to do it. I closed my eyes and told him I was stressed and that I needed to do my deep breathing. He went quiet and then went to his bedroom saying 'You've gone mad'. But he didn't go on and on like he normally does. It made me feel so good.*

Islay: *I remember you said that you are loud and people think you are angry when you're not. I'm wondering if you are managing to focus that strength in a more positive way.*

Paris: *I hadn't thought of it like that, but yes I do say what I think,* my friends say I can be quite scary. Maybe I haven't been using my strength in the best way.

Kim: *Margaret how did you get on? Did you manage to move outside of your comfort zone?*

Margaret: *Well, I left here really determined, but as soon as I got home Damien was moaning about me being late. I started to apologise but then I remembered about the familiar zone so I ignored his questioning and told him what a great time I'd had. I got the impression that he'd been a bit scared and I was wondering whether he gets that from me. My mum was at home with him but I think he worries about me when I am out.*

Kim: *Our children do worry about us and we need to reassure them that we are okay. We will look at the reasons for that later on in this session.*

Angie: *Harry is absolutely fine at school and the teachers can't believe I am describing the same child. He's bright and polite and never answers back. So I started to think about why he is so difficult with me. I realise now that my love for him may be getting in the way of what is best for him. It was when Paris said about always believing Riley that made me stop and think. I think that's what I do with Harry. He's just so precious to me that I worry all the time that something will happen to him. I have been thinking that this could be a bit suffocating for him.*

Darren: *I feel a bit like that with Mikki. She's my only child. I know I push her to be the best and I can see that she gets fed up with me. I think it is important to have standards though.*

Anne: *I have noticed a difference. You seem to be more patient with Mikki and you have started to treat her more like an eight-year-old. I know that sometimes I expect her to be older too. I guess* that's because I have the older children and it's easy to forget at times that she is only eight.

Martin: I don't know about it all. It's just such a struggle. I have four children and it's manic getting them ready for school and nursery. I have to get on at them otherwise nothing will happen. I tell them what to do but they dawdle. They'd rather watch TV than get dressed in the morning.

Angie looks a bit taken aback.

Angie: When Harry was younger he was so awful at getting ready for school that I banned TV in the morning. I felt really bad about saying it and he didn't like it but it changed things for the better. At first he would refuse to get himself dressed, so someone told me about using a timer and we'd have a race to see who could get dressed first. He loved it, as he would usually win.

Martin: I hadn't thought of doing that. I might give it a go although they'll probably just start arguing about who's going to win.

Martin heaves a big sigh. He is really struggling with the lack of space at home and the different ages of his children.

Islay: In this session we are going to look at all the influences on our behaviour. This includes all of the information we take in, the messages we receive about ourselves and the family habits and traditions that have been handed down to us by our family. I hope that this session will help you to think about where some of your behaviour may come from. We will link this session back to the Window to Self-Knowledge and Comfort, Stretch, Panic. To understand why we behave the way we do let's go back to the very beginning. When babies are born how do they communicate with their parents?

Margaret: *By crying?*

Islay: *Yes. The only way that your newborn baby can communicate with you is by crying. The crying tells you that your baby is uncomfortable in some way, and you will respond to the crying and make your baby comfortable. After a few weeks how else do they communicate with you?*

Paris: *Babies start to smile and gurgle.*

Islay: *Yes, they start to learn other ways to communicate, they start to smile, gurgle and use baby talk. How have they learnt this?*

Martin: *It's because they've copied us.*

Islay: *Yes, a baby copies the behaviour that is shown towards them; they learn their responses through watching others. This is called learnt behaviour.*

Paris: *I've never thought of it like that. So they copy what we do?*

Islay: *Yes, they do. Children are like sponges, they take in the information they receive from their parents and families, and this is how they learn. Our children are absorbing our words and actions all of the time.*

Kim: *One way to understand behaviour is to think about what we, as parents, have been shown and also what behaviour we are showing to our children. There is a short clip of an advert on YouTube. It is called* Children see, children do *(https://www.youtube.com/ watch?v=KHi2dxSf9hw). It was NAPCAN's TV advert shown in Australia, which was used to promote a child-friendly Australia. It illustrates really well how children copy their parents' behaviour. It focuses on negative behaviour, but it does end with some positives demonstrating that we have the power to choose our responses.*

The clip is shown and as it stops there is silence in the room.

Angie: *That's made me sad, and I feel like crying.*

Margaret: *Yes, it's made me think about what I may be passing on to Damien. I'm nervous and anxious and I'm starting to see that in him.*

Kim: *Often the images from this film can shock parents but it can also help them to think about what they are teaching their children. There were some strong images there and it showed how children copy what they see.*

Islay: *The images in the film are shocking, they are actions and therefore more obvious than the spoken word. The words that we say to our children are just as powerful. We will be looking at communication in a later session but for now I would like you to think about the messages that have been handed down to you and the messages that you may be handing down to your children.*

The parents are looking thoughtful and very serious. This could be the first time that they have thought about how their behaviour impacts on their child.

Paris: *I feel really awful now. I don't even realise what I am saying to Riley most of the time. I know how he speaks to me though and that's like I'm a piece of dirt. I just want him to be good and do what he should be doing. I've tried everything. Shouting at him, pleading with him, all he does is push me away.*

Kim: *What did you hear when you were growing up Paris?*

Paris: *That I was crap. My mum was always telling my dad that I was trouble and that she couldn't handle me. I would never say that about Riley, I know what that feels like. I am going to stand by him whatever happens.*

Islay: *Thank you for sharing that, Paris. The messages that are passed on can be said to us or said about us. They can be passed on through other comments such as 'You won't be able to do that' – you're stupid – or 'You can do anything you want to' – you're clever.*

Kim: *We can relate this to the behaviour in Box 3 and Box 4 of the Window to Self-Knowledge. The messages you have received are like secret orders that have been given to you in a sealed envelope and stored in Box 4. If you don't think about why you behave the way you do, you are acting on these orders without knowing what they are.*

Islay: *We will have picked up messages about ourselves and the way to behave from our parents. Can anyone think of a time when they have behaved like or sounded like their parents?*

Angie: *Oh don't. I was horrified the other day when Harry had a smudge on his face and without thinking I got a tissue, spat on it and went to rub the mark off his face. I just managed to stop myself. That was what my mum used to do to me and as a child I absolutely hated it. And then I found myself doing it.*

Angie shudders as the memory returns.

---

**What am I teaching my child? Pick up the mirror and take a look at your own behaviour. Ask 'By behaving in this way what am I teaching my child?' Are you happy with the answer? If the answer is no then it is time to change your behaviour.**

---

Islay: *As well as our parents there are other influences on us. This is the information that we are bombarded with on a daily basis. Can you tell me what influences there are on our children?*

Angie: *School gives them loads of information.*

Paris: *And then there's the internet and television. A lot of it is good but I do worry sometimes what Riley is looking at on the internet. You know what boys are like ….*

Margaret: *For me it's Damien's friends. I worry sometimes about what they are encouraging him to do.*

Islay: *It's hard for parents because there is information that you have no control over. And you have even less control as they get older. If you also take into account advertising, the media, plus the influence of any activities and clubs that your child belongs to, that is a lot of influences. Much of this will be positive, but as parents we need to set boundaries around how much information and the kinds of information our children receive. We also need to think about the information we are passing onto them.*

Kim: *Of course as adults we receive all of this information as well, but instead of it coming from school it may come from work and it also comes from our children.*

Paris: *'I hate you' comes to mind.*

Martin: *Yeah, or 'You never buy me anything I want'.*

All of the parents in the group nod in agreement.

Islay: *Because we are bombarded with lots of information our brains can't cope with it all, so we have learnt to filter out what is not important to us and to keep what we feel is important. If we didn't have these filters we would become overloaded. It would be impossible to function as there would be too much going on. For each one of us, what we think is important will be different.*

Martin: *So are you saying that what happens to us in our lives will determine what we discard and what we keep? That sounds a bit scary?*

Islay: *It's not all bad. But, as with everything, if we don't spend the time working out what is going on then we will just keep behaving the way we always have. We gather information over time and it starts as soon as we are born. There is on-going research into stress and the effect it has on the unborn child, which implies that information is gathered as soon as we are conceived. As we grow from babies to adults we will develop our filters based on the experiences we are provided with. These filters continue to develop throughout our life, and they will affect us in positive or negative ways.*

Kim: *We can relate the use of filters to the present day where you will only pay attention to the information that is important to you. It's a bit like deciding which TV programmes that you want to watch; there are hundreds of channels but you will choose the ones that you want to pay attention to.*

Islay: *The filters happen on a conscious level and on a subconscious level. The conscious level is where you notice specific information. If something suddenly becomes important to you it will become more noticeable. If you are thinking about buying a particular make of car you will suddenly start to see lots of them around. This doesn't mean that they weren't there before it means that they weren't important to you before.*

Anne: *Wow, that's just like when I was pregnant I kept seeing pregnant women everywhere I went.*

Paris: *Yeah, me too. Riley keeps pointing out kids wearing the trainers that he wants me to buy him, it seems like everyone has them.*

Islay: *When the filters happen subconsciously it is outside of your awareness. This again links back to the Window to Self-Knowledge, Box 3 and Box 4. If we received lots of negative messages about ourselves when we were growing up, our filtering system will discard the positive and will just let in the negative. However, if the messages we received were positive our filtering system will be more likely to filter out the negative and to let in the positive.*

Anne: *Is that like the saying 'Is your glass half full or is your glass half empty?'? Mine is often half empty.*

Angie: *And I am the opposite. I like to look at things in a positive way.*

Islay: *Yes and it relates back to the view of the world that our parents have passed onto us. Imagine a large kitchen sink and the sink has a plug in it. The tap however is slowly dripping. After a long period of time the sink will slowly fill up. Imagine you are that kitchen sink and the drips from the tap are the messages you have received as a child. If those messages were positive ones such as, you are valued, loved and wanted, then the occasional negative message will not have much impact. However, if for example you were constantly told, you are a pain in the neck, you are stupid, you were a mistake, you would be receiving negative messages. In this case the occasional positive message will not have much impact, as the underpinning message is negative.*

Paris looks as if she's about to cry.

Paris: *I said earlier that I'd never say about Riley to others what my mum used to say to my dad about me. But now I remember I was so upset with him recently that I told him he was useless and would never amount to anything. I feel so awful.*

Islay: *Paris, I understand you feel awful, but it's at this point all of us have choices. None of us are perfect parents and we all get it wrong and say things we shouldn't at times. That wouldn't have been a nice thing for Riley to hear. However the important thing now is to change the overall message you are giving to your child. We need to find another way of teaching them so they recognise it's their behaviour that is wrong, not them.*

**Ask for your child's opinion.** When we ask our children for their opinion the message we are giving them is that they are important and we value them.

Kim: *So we have looked at information we receive and how we use filters to manage it. We have looked at how this impacts on both our children and ourselves. There is one more piece to the puzzle of our behaviour and this is our family habits. Through the generations of our family we pass on family habits such as values, expectations, and beliefs. These habits are handed down outside of our awareness and they become our automatic behaviour. Unless we question them as adults we will continue to act upon them regardless of whether they are working for us or against us.*

**Positive Habits: Positive habits come from parents who show consistent and appropriate boundaries and love. Given this experience you would expect good things to happen to you, you are able to trust others and have respect for boundaries, yours and others'. This creates a helpful outlook on life and will have given you the ability to develop to your full potential.**

> **Negative Habits: Negative habits come from your parent being unable to provide consistent and appropriate boundaries and love. Given this experience you may expect bad things to happen to you, you may have no trust in others and have little respect for your own boundaries or others' boundaries. This creates an unhelpful outlook on life, one with few goals and expectations and you would be less likely to reach your full potential.**

Islay: *As with our filters, our habits can be conscious or subconscious, out of our awareness. Can anyone give an example of a family habit or tradition that they are consciously aware of?*

Angie: *When we were growing up Sunday lunch was really important and it didn't matter what we were up to during the week we all had to be at home for Sunday lunch. It was always a roast dinner and we sat and talked. It was a really precious time and I have carried that on. Our children know how important it is to be there for Sunday lunch. Harry is beginning to rebel against it and we do end up having rows about it but I absolutely insist he is there for Sunday lunch.*

Islay: *That's a great example. Is anyone now aware of a family habit or tradition that they were once unaware of?*

There is silence in the room.

Kim: *I read something that my granddaughter had written at school that fits in here. She had been asked to write about her family and she had written that every year on Christmas Eve we all go bowling. When I read it I realised that it was a family tradition, something we did every year and it was something that we all enjoyed. I hadn't thought about it as a tradition, but it is a tradition to her.*

Paris: *I don't really understand the difference between a family tradition and a family habit?*

Islay: *It's complicated as really they are both habits, which just means you keep doing them. However a tradition is a conscious act and will have a meaning behind it. You might do something in remembrance of someone and it might be on a particular day each year or it might be something you do for religious reasons, like saying grace before a meal. A habit is something that happens just because it has always been done that way. When examined there might not be a reason behind it and there might not be good enough reasons to continue to do it.*

Anne: *Is that like my Nan? She fell out with her sister and they never made up. My mum always talks down about that side of the family. Recently I asked her why and she didn't know.*

Islay: *Yes, and isn't it sad. That has been carried over and nobody knows why. But well done for asking the question to your mum because that might make her think and, who knows, it could start a reconciliation.*

Kim: *As an adult, by looking at the Window to Self-Knowledge you can work out whether your filters and habits are working for you or against you. You could ask for feedback from your friends and coming to a group like this, where other people are talking about their situations will help. When we listen to others talking we try to make sense of what we are hearing by comparing their situation to ours. Has anyone started to question their own behaviour since they have heard others in the group talking?*

Margaret: *Yes I have. I have been thinking about where my fear and anxiety might be coming from. My mother constantly worried about everything. My dad would tell her everything would be all right but she could see fears around every corner. I used to get angry with her and when I was young I was a nightmare. I think back to that time and I realise I have lost the independent person I used to be. Paris has helped me as she's so strong and doesn't seem frightened of anything.*

Paris looks really surprised.

Paris: *I don't see myself as the person you've just described. I get angry and then everything goes wrong for me. I'm beginning to look back and think about what has made me so angry. I had a pretty awful upbringing and got pregnant at 15. It was my way of escaping and I thought finally I have someone to love me.*

Islay: *It seems like you have started to understand more about the way you behave now by examining your past. How you react or respond to a situation depends on what you notice – filters – and what you expect to happen – habits – and this will have come from your past experiences.*

Kim: *We can link this back to the comfort, stretch, panic zones, from Session 1. If the information you receive is what you expect or if it is familiar to you then you will stay in your comfort zone. If the information you receive is not what you are used to then you will feel unsafe and move into the stretch or panic zone.*

Islay: *One of the challenges of attempting to change our behaviour is moving out of our comfort zone. As much as we say we want things to change, our desire to stay in our comfort zone is stronger. This can keep us stuck in our well-established patterns of behaviour, the patterns that our children are used to.*

Kim: *It is a challenge to move into the stretch zone but this is where the learning takes place and where change happens. This is where you create new patterns of behaviour. We are going to do an exercise now in pairs to explore with each other what your habits and filters may be preventing you from doing.*

The group moves and there is a real hub of noise as they start to share with each other some of their experiences and how they may be helping or hindering their relationship with their children. Kim writes the following questions on a flip chart:

> **Identify one habit or filter.**
> **Where has that come from?**
> **Is it working for you or against you?**

After a few minutes Kim asks the group to come back. She asks them if that was helpful and did they manage to identify anything they need to look at.

Martin: *I found that hard. I was talking with Darren and he was really helpful. This sort of thing is not something that blokes normally like doing but we both like football so it was a bit easier. We decided that a family habit could be which football team you support. I support the same team that my dad supported and John supports them as well. However Jessie is mad about football and says our team is useless and she supports another team. I really struggle with Jessie and sometimes I think she says things to wind me up. I've realised that it was really important to me that we all support the same team and I was trying to pass that onto the children. What I see now is that it's okay for Jessie to support whatever team she wants to support and we can have some good competition when the teams are playing against each other. I guess it's not as important to her to follow the family habit and although that is hard for me to accept I need to find a way to make this work for us all.*

Kim: *That's a wonderful acknowledgement. If we allow our children to make their own decisions then life becomes much happier. It's recognising that you and your child are different people. What is* important to you might not be important to them. We do need to ask ourselves 'Is this stance so important to me that I am willing to put my relationship with my child at risk?'

Islay: *Another challenge we face when we attempt to change our behaviour is our memories. When you are faced with a situation you will subconsciously ask yourself whether you have experienced this before, and what did you do last time. Your memories tell you what is safe for you and what is unsafe. If your memories tell you that you are unsafe you may be triggered into the panic zone. Our fear of moving out of our comfort zone can keep us stuck in old patterns of behaviour.*

Kim: *Self-awareness is crucial to making changes to our behaviour, the more aware we are of why we behave the way we do the easier it is to learn new patterns of behaviour. How you react or respond to a situation depends on what you notice – filters – and what you expect to happen – habits; the best thing you can do for yourself and your child is to learn more about your filters, your habits and your trigger points, so you can work out those situations or memories that send you into the panic zone.*

The time has run out for Session 3 and Kim is interested to hear what the parents are taking away from this session.

Martin: *I like the idea of the timer that Angie suggested and I'll try that.*

Anne: *A lot of information and some food for thought. I feel like this session has been a stretch for me, taken me out of my comfort zone, but I'm not sure why.*

Angie: *I need to think about what I do for Harry and whether I'm suffocating him. There were some things that have been said today that make me wonder. It's made me feel uncomfortable.*

Margaret: *The DVD had a big effect on me. It was shocking, but it has really shown me how Damien may be learning ways of behaving from me.*

Islay: *During the week try to notice what behaviour you are paying attention to and whether it is positive or negative.*

There was an unusual quiet in the room as the parents left the session to return to their daily lives. The DVD clip was hard hitting and the mood in the room suggested that the parents had been affected. Paris was in good spirits as she stood up and made her way towards the door. Most of her life it had seemed like other people had only bad things to say about her. They had said that she was loud and aggressive, well maybe that is how it looked. She had fought her way through life, there had been no one for her to turn to other than Riley; he had been her rock. As she left the room Paris had renewed enthusiasm. She thought about asking Riley what he thought their family traditions were and guessed what his answer would be.

Darren was finding it hard to think straight. His life had changed massively since he had become a dad; it wasn't quite what he expected. He certainly didn't expect to be coming to a parenting group and he wasn't finding it very helpful to be talking about his failings. Anne seemed to be too quick to point them out to the others in the group. He was really trying to be patient with Mikki but she was pushing him to the limit. It hadn't always been like this between him and Anne. When they had first met she had leaned on him, trusted him to make decisions and to look after her. Darren wondered what she trusted him to do now, and how long it would take to get things back to normal.

 **Exercise** gives you time to think things through and clear your mind.

## OWL WISDOM

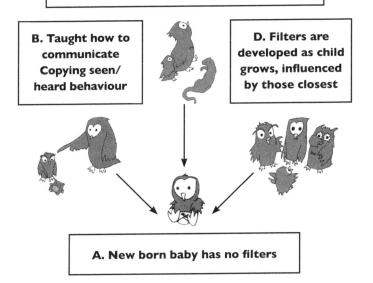

**C. Family habits, values, expectations and beliefs lead to helpful/unhelpful messages**

**B. Taught how to communicate Copying seen/ heard behaviour**

**D. Filters are developed as child grows, influenced by those closest**

**A. New born baby has no filters**

This diagram illustrates how we receive and interpret information throughout our lives. It shows the many influences that define our judgments and values. Picture A shows that a baby is born with no filters. Initially they develop these through their parents, siblings and wider family. As they grow there are other outside influences upon them. Picture B demonstrates the mother owl pointing at her child. The child is learning a pattern of behaviour, which is then repeated to the teddy. Picture C illustrates the parent giving an unhelpful message to their child. The mother owl is turning her nose up at the weasel and the child is copying her. Picture D shows the importance of belonging in a family. A child learns whether they are loved and valued from the messages they receive as they grow. The judgments our parents make will affect our behaviour as this gives us permission to think the same. As parents this will include our attitudes to the following: education, work, single parents, or to anyone who is different from us.

Importantly, as a child grows into an adult these judgments and values will continue unless their relevance and appropriateness are questioned. As parents we have a responsibility to ensure that the messages we give our children are balanced. We can only achieve this by being self-aware. As parents we have a responsibility to ensure that the messages we give our children are balanced. We can only achieve this by being self-aware.

 ## FOR REFLECTION

1. Can you identify a family *habit* that you have? Is it a positive or negative *habit?*

2. Do you know what your family traditions are? Ask your child/children what they think your family traditions are.

3. What are your expectations for your child/children regarding the following:
   • Education
   • Lifestyle
   • Goals
   • Relationships.

4. What are your expectations for yourself regarding the following:
   • Work
   • Lifestyle
   • Goals
   • Relationships.

5. What have you learned in this chapter that will help you to behave differently when your child is being violent?

# 4

# THE NECESSITIES
# OF LIFE

 **Have fun together.** Make a list of fun activities; include things that are free, things that cost small amounts of money and things that cost larger amounts of money.

The weekly phone call showed that most of the parents were struggling. When parents start to make changes their child is likely to resist and their behaviour gets worse; the parents can then feel like they have hit a brick wall. Parents may give up on the new behaviour and revert to old patterns. This is when some will feel like dropping out of the group. At this stage the support of the group becomes vital.

Kim: *Is anyone willing to share one thing that has gone right this week?*

Martin: *I tried the timer for getting dressed. It didn't work so I got fed up with it and stopped doing it.*

Margaret: *I've been feeling a bit miserable and Damien has been playing up. We have had some shouting matches. I've tried to be more positive but it has been impossible.*

Paris: *I've been feeling okay this week. If Riley started I've said 'Yeah, whatever' and walked away. Normally I'd snap back.*

Islay: *What you've described is how our feelings impact on how we behave. It's not about stopping the feelings, as they are important, it's about not being totally motivated by them. We will look more deeply at feelings in another session.*

Anne: *My friend helped me with this one. She said: 'Imagine you are going shopping and you are feeling miserable. You have had a row with your children and a bill has come through the letterbox that you can't pay. As you are pushing your shopping trolley, by accident you hit someone's legs. They turn angrily to you and say 'Oi, look where you're going, idiot!' As you're already upset you're more likely to have a shouting match. My friend then said to me. Imagine instead that you have just won the lottery and you are going round the supermarket with your trolley and the same thing happens.*

The group laugh and together agree they'd say instead, 'Sorry, let me buy your shopping for you'.

Kim: *Let's look at some other factors involved in our behaviour patterns. One way to unpick these patterns is to recognise that all behaviour is designed to meet an underlying need. When it comes to understanding behaviour it is important to see that there is a vast difference between a want and a need. In a lot of ways the media and advertising will convince you that you want things that you are unable to afford. Your children may also manipulate you into giving them everything they want. This is quite different from the fundamental needs that lie underneath our behaviour. Can anyone think what their child might want instead of need?*

Margaret: *Damien wants new trainers. I know he needs a pair but he's insisting on the most expensive pair in the shop. I can't afford them.*

Martin: *I find John's friends difficult but he goes on about how much he needs to see them.*

Islay: *Your child's view of what they need will be determined by what everyone else has got or what they see in the media. Having their needs met is something completely different.*

Kim: *One way that we can make sense of this is linking what we need, rather than what we want, to our behaviour patterns. We can start to see that the way we behave is a way of getting our needs met. Several needs are often met through one of our behaviours. What we will discover is that our needs can be met in either positive or negative ways, and that is true for both you and your child.*

Islay: *There is a way of looking at our needs which we can use which fits around the word **S.A.F.E.R.**. The first one is **Self-sufficiency**, which is about being independent. It is having confidence in your own abilities and feeling good about yourself. Being self-sufficient is about being open to challenge and being able to recognise when you need to change. It is welcoming new ideas and being prepared to learn. To become self-sufficient it helps if you have people around you who care about you and take an interest in your life.*

Kim: *The next need is **Autonomy**, which is having a sense of control in our lives. It is feeling confident that you will be listened to and that your thoughts and feelings are valued. It helps you to achieve autonomy if you have people around you who understand you and who are prepared to listen to what you have to say.*

Islay: *The next need is **Fitting in** which relates to our sense of belonging; we all need to feel like we belong somewhere, like we are part of something. This relates to being connected to others; we need people to be pleased to see us and to want to be in our company. We also need to feel that we are making a contribution to society. You feel like you belong when you have* *people around you who show you that you are valued and that they care about you.*

Kim: *The next need is* **Enjoyment** *and this is one need that is often forgotten about. The need to have fun and to have things to look forward to provides a feeling of excitement. It is important to have people around you who share a sense of enjoyment in life. Enjoyment releases endorphins and this gives a sense of wellbeing.*

Islay: *The final need is* **Respect**, *which relates to our need for attention, appreciation and consideration. In many ways this need is a thread running through the other needs. Respect is how you are treated and how you treat others. The SAFER needs are related to 'what' we do, while respect is related to 'how' we do it. We don't always think about whether we give or receive respect but we miss it when it is not there. It is important to have people around you who respect you so that you feel loved, trusted and valued.*

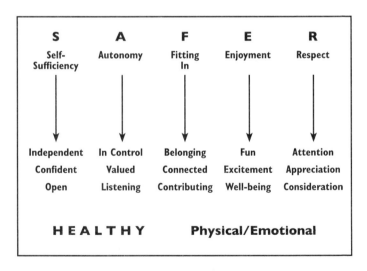

Kim: *Margaret, you talked about Damien wanting new trainers. Any idea what need that might be meeting?*

Martin: *They have to have trainers. Mine are always saying that they need new ones. They seem to wear them out so quickly.*

Margaret: *Damien says all his friends have got the ones that he wants and that he'll be left out if he doesn't have them.*

Paris: *Riley tries that one on but then he doesn't go to school very often so he doesn't even see his friends.*

Anne: *My older boys used to be like that. It was like they were trying to fit in, but I think it was also about doing things their way and testing out their power. That must come under Autonomy.*

Islay: *I wonder if this is about confidence. If you are feeling confident about yourself then it won't matter what trainers you are wearing. However, if you have low self-confidence then external things become much more important.*

Kim: *This isn't just about our children. It's also about us. We also need to get our own needs met in SAFER ways so I'm wondering how confident you all feel about yourselves?*

Margaret: *I always worry about making a decision. I always think I'm going to make the wrong one.*

Islay: *Margaret, you have been really self-aware in the group and the first part of change is recognition. Next time you have self-doubt what do you think you could do differently?*

Margaret: *I don't know. Each week I say I'm going to change and nothing happens. Damien still has violent episodes and I am so ashamed.*

Kim: *Sometimes there's a voice in our head telling us how useless or stupid we are, especially if we think we have got something wrong.*

The group members nod and agree that happens a lot.

Kim: *At some point we need to change the voice to a different one. Margaret, what could you change that voice to?*

Margaret: *I don't know. I hate the sound of my own voice. Maybe I could change it to a cartoon character?*

Kim: *Good. Which one?*

Anne: *What about Tigger from Winnie-the-Pooh? He's always upbeat.*

Martin: *I say to Jessie to think about Donkey from* Shrek. *It makes her laugh so if she's feeling down she says it helps.*

Margaret: *I love that. I'm going to think about Donkey from now on.*

Islay: *Thinking about SAFER how do you think your children are getting their needs met? This will be different for children depending on their age. Let's get into your pairs to discuss this.*

The parents soon begin to realise that they all parent their children differently. Margaret does almost everything for Damien and Paris lets Riley do most things for himself. Paris is horrified that Margaret is still doing everything for Damien, including choosing what clothes he wears. Margaret is surprised by Paris's almost lack of care towards Riley. When the parents return to the larger group Angie shares what she has learned.

Angie: *It seems to me that there should be both support and independence. If there is too much just one way, whether it is support or independence, then a child won't get what they need.*

Islay draws the image of some weighing scales and expands on Angie's point.

Islay: *It's a good point that you have made, Angie; a good balance is so important. For children to grow and feel safe they need to be allowed to make decisions for themselves. They need to be given reasonable choices. They need to learn to do things for themselves and when things go wrong, as they sometimes will; they need to be able to solve things themselves. It's vital they find ways of solving their own problems. This will build their self-confidence.*

Kim: *We said earlier that the need for enjoyment is sometimes overlooked. Can anyone tell me when they last had fun with their child? What did you do?*

Martin: *Last week we went to the park to fly a kite. John didn't want to come and I said okay, but if he was staying at home then he needed to clean up his side of the room. He didn't want to do that so he came as well. We had a great time and he was really good with Kyle.*

Angie: *I'm going to try Martin's suggestion about geocaching this weekend. Philip is really looking forward to it and has already downloaded the app. Harry's really excited and it's so lovely to hear them planning it.*

 **Say sorry.** It will help your child realise that it's okay to get things wrong and it's not the end of the world. Failing doesn't make you a failure.

Islay: *That's a really good example of offering fun times and perservering when your child is resistant, thank you Martin and Angie. We will keep coming back to this one as we go through the sessions It is really important to have fun together. Let's link what we have talked about today, which is how we get our needs met, to what we have learnt previously.*

Islay refers back to the Window to Self-Knowledge:

Islay: *If you are meeting your needs in positive ways then you are probably in Box I of the Window to Self-Knowledge. Most of the time you would feel loved, cared for and appreciated. You would be listening to yourself and others, be quite confident about the decisions that you make and feel in control of your life. You would be able to have fun and get excited about the future.*

Kim: *If your needs are being met in a negative way you are more likely to be in Box 2, 3 and 4. Remember if you are in these two boxes your behaviour is outside of your awareness, your blind and hidden area, so you will be meeting your needs but it may be in negative ways. You may be in denial about the reasons behind your behaviour and be stuck in familiar patterns of behaviour. Other people may have tried to tell you about your behaviour but you may find that you get defensive and refuse to hear it. Equally you may behave in a secretive way and justify your actions because it's not hurting anyone. Your needs will still be met but in a negative way.*

Islay: *We have looked at what needs we have, SAFER, and that we behave in certain ways in order to get these needs met. The next step is to start to recognise whether the need is being met in positive ways or negative ways. Positive ways will enable you to build good relationships and achieve great things. Negative ways will hold you back and will eventually increase your anger.*

Martin: *It all seems a bit confusing. Am I right that everything we do will be meeting a need in some way or another? So if I go out for a drink with my mates the need I'm meeting is fun and enjoyment?*

Darren: *Could you also be meeting the need for belonging and attention?*

Anne: *That's all very well until you come home drunk and then someone has to clean up after you. That's not being very respectful to me.*

Paris: *Sounds like that also could meet a need. Someone to clean up after you to show they care.*

The group laughs. Anne, though, is left wondering if there is any truth behind that. Darren is a lot younger than she is and he still wants to be one of the lads. He doesn't seem to want to take responsibility for anything. Anne has a thoughtful expression on her face, which may be leading her towards a lightbulb moment.

 **Keep things light.** Humour used wisely can change the mood.

Kim: *As you can see it can get quite complicated. It is impossible to change anyone else's behaviour, but it is worth taking some time to think about how you might be meeting other people's needs when really that is their responsibility.*

Anne: *I've had a thought. When Sophie was younger she used to forget her PE kit all the time. I would rush up to the school to take it to her so that she wouldn't get a detention. I suppose she didn't have to take responsibility because I rescued her. So from what we have seen today she was getting attention and it gave her a sense of belonging. She knew that I cared about her, and in a funny sort of way it made me feel needed. So my need for belonging was being met.*

Kim: *And now looking back would you say that these were positive or negative ways of getting needs met?*

Anne: *I suppose a bit of both. It's nice to do things for your children and it's okay for it to make you feel good as well. The problem was Sophie always expected me to do it and if I reminded her about the PE kit she'd get cross and start shouting at me. It got really awful and I started to resent her for making me do it.*

Islay: *It's interesting that you've said she made you do it. Can anyone make us do anything Anne? Is there anything else you could have done?*

Anne: *Well, if I hadn't taken it in for her she would have got a detention. I didn't want that. I think what you're saying is that I should have let her have a detention so that she learnt for herself. It's probably true, but hard to do.*

Kim: *At times like this it helps to think 'Whose problem is it?' Would it have been your problem if Sophie had got a detention or would it have been Sophie's problem?*

Anne: *Again a bit of both. The detentions were after school and I wouldn't have been able to get back to pick her up. So it was just easier for me to rescue her all the time.*

Kim: *What were you teaching her, Anne?*

Anne squirms and looks uncomfortable.

Anne: *That I would always pick up the pieces for her … and I still do.*

Islay: *Well done Anne, that's good insight. It's very tempting in these situations to get stuck in the 'either/or' mentalities where we think we only have two choices. I'm wondering if anyone has any other choices for Anne. Is there anything else she could have done?*

Margaret: *When Damien was getting detentions after school I found it really helpful to talk to his teacher. Damien's teacher suggested that if it happened again they would give him the detention in the lunch break. I told Damien that and now he knows that it's up to him and he will have the consequence not me.*

Kim introduces an exercise to help the parents recognise how their children's needs are being met. She asks the parents to write a list of positive ways of meeting needs and a list of negative ways of meeting needs. The group produces the following lists:

---

**POSITIVE WAYS OF MEETING NEEDS**
**Allowing them choices**
**Asking their opinion**
**Listening to them**
**Allowing flexibility**
**Having fun time as a family**
**Recognising and saying when things go well**
**Looking for the positives**
**Giving them responsibility (age appropriate)**
**Making clear the consequence of their actions and
    sticking to it**
**Allowing them to get involved**
**Friends**
**Finding a hobby.**

---

**NEGATIVE WAYS OF MEETING NEEDS**
**Ignoring them**
**Shouting**
**Getting into arguments**
**Being sarcastic**
**Teasing them in a nasty way**
**Putting them down in front of their friends**
**Telling them they'll never amount to anything**
**Getting angry with them**
**Refusing to trust them**
**Use of drugs and alcohol**
**Friends.**

Kim refers to the negative ways of meeting needs list:

Kim: *If someone was experiencing getting their needs met in a negative way, how do you think they would behave?*

Paris: *That sounds like my childhood. I used to be really rude and I thought that if no one cared about me then I didn't care about them. I was angry with everyone and very suspicious of anyone who was nice to me. Nobody ever said well done to me or if they did I didn't hear it. I was always so angry.*

Kim: *That sounds pretty tough for you. What do you think would have been different if your needs had been met in positive ways?*

Paris: *I don't know. I might not be so strong but maybe I wouldn't feel as if everyone is against me and I have to fight all the time.*

Margaret: *I was never valued when I was younger and it made me really insecure as if I was never good enough. I'm beginning to realise that I don't want that for Damien. I really need to think about what I am passing onto him in a negative way and think about how I can turn that around so he learns that life doesn't have to be frightening. It's hard though when you doubt yourself all the time.*

Angie: *I think you are amazing, Margaret. You really think things through. I do hope you succeed. I don't think you need to be scared because you have managed so well. Damien is lucky to have you as a mum.*

Margaret gets a bit upset. It's clear that this is the first time that someone has praised her openly and she has heard it without denying it.

Angie: *I was thinking about Enjoyment and how that need might get met in negative ways. It might be the same for adults as well as children. I was thinking that it could be met by being in relationships that aren't very good for us. That would also link into Autonomy where a child, or adult, might say 'You can't tell me what to do I can be friends with whoever I want'. I was interested to see that friends were in both lists. It made me think about my friends and whether they are good for me. Do they give me positive messages or do they drag me down?*

Paris: *And Fitting in could be like when Riley is trying to be one of the crowd. A lot of the kids near us get into drugs, drinking alcohol and offending. I have warned him that he'd better not end up like that. I heard one of his friends say to another one, 'You did well nicking that stuff, you walked right past the security guard, well done'. I hadn't thought of this but I suppose you would say he was getting his needs met for Fitting in but in a negative way.*

Kim: *Some brilliant examples there, thank you. Friends can be so important and rather than focus on whether you think their friends are a bad influence on them, think, as Angie is doing, whether* your friends are a good influence on you. Equally are you a good influence on them?

Islay: *What about self-sufficiency can anyone give an example of that one?*

Martin: *Is that when you don't take help, trying to do things in your own way, but struggling to be totally self-sufficient.*

Islay: *Yes, this is about the extremes once again.*

Martin: *Well that's John. He gets so stressed with schoolwork but won't let me help, and I suppose it's me, trying to manage the kids on my own.*

Islay: *What do you think John is hearing when you say to him let me help you?*

Martin: *That I think he can't do it on his own?*

Islay: *So how else might you be able to say to him that you'd like to help?*

Martin: *Well I suppose I could stop telling him that he's getting it all wrong and just let him know that I'd like to help if he wants me to. That might make him more open to some help.*

Kim: *If someone is trying to force their help on you it can make you feel as if you can't do it and that you're going to fail. If you're given an opportunity to try it first and then you struggle, it's easier to go to someone who'll help without making you feel that you're a nuisance. All of us need encouragement when we are trying something difficult. We may not need to give our children the answers just listen to the fact that they are finding it a struggle.*

Islay: *So this leads us on nicely to Respect.*

Paris: *What respect … Kids don't seem to have any today.*

Darren: *I had no respect for anyone when I was growing up.*

Islay: *It's an interesting thing, respect. We all want to be treated with respect but have we thought about how we get it and whether we respect other people?*

Paris: *I treat everyone decently until they go against me and then that's it. They don't deserve another chance.*

Angie: *Oh dear, I think that's how wars start….*

Paris: *Yes, it does feel like a war sometimes.*

Islay: *So if we want respect what do we need to do to get it?*

Martin: *I think I'm beginning to see that if we give like for like in a negative way then nothing will change, it will just continue.*

Kim: *Yes, that is hugely important. Most parents want their child to change. After all they are the ones being violent. However they are still children and aren't able to work through and process their emotions. It is up to us as the adults to look at what we can do differently. Then change will happen.*

Islay: *One way that you can make positive changes happen is to meet those needs at home in positive ways. It doesn't mean ignoring the negative behaviour because clearly if your child is being threatening to you, you have to deal with it.*

Margaret: *I don't feel I have any control over Damien. He just does what he likes.*

Paris: *I feel the same about Riley, he can be so aggressive.*

Kim: *As our children get older they demand more independence, which can be really hard for parents, especially when their children show challenging behaviour.*

Anne: *When my first husband died so suddenly it was a real shock for all of us. The children withdrew from me. It was as if they blamed me in some strange way. They got so angry. Then, when I met Darren, they got even angrier. They were pretty awful to you, Darren.*

Darren: *Yes they were. They really resented me. I think they were afraid they were going to lose you as well.*

Anne: *Yes, I recognised that they were scared. That underneath their behaviour they were feeling hurt, sad, and abandoned, first by their dad and then possibly by me. It was such a difficult time for us all. I found it hard to meet their needs and I know it sounds awful but I just had to find a way to survive.*

Angie: *How soon did you and Darren get together after your husband died?*

Anne: *It was nine months. Darren became my rock. I couldn't have coped without him. I still have difficulty with my older three; things can be quite strained. Peter still lives at home. I know he wants to move out but he can't afford it. He spends most of his time in his room when he's at home and he won't join in when we ask him. He gets cross with Mikki and tells us we give in too much to her.*

Islay: *Anne, you've mentioned some really strong feelings there: hurt, sadness and abandoned. If you were feeling like that, what would you have needed? What would have made it better for you?*

Anne: *I'm not sure. I guess those things that we put on the flip chart paper. Being listened to, having my feelings recognised, being included in things, being given choices, feeling supported. Although I try to do that with my older ones the message doesn't seem to get through.*

Kim: *What do you think is getting in the way?*

Margaret: *For me it's because if I don't get the immediate response that I need, then I get upset. I've tried to change some of these things with Damien but he looks at me as if I'm stupid, that's when I curl up inside. I find it so hard to stay calm. I then either scream and shout or walk away and ignore him. I'm again wondering if this is more about me than Damien.*

Kim: *Our children do go through different stages. They think their parents know nothing. They roll their eyes and it can be infuriating. This is normal. However, if our need for attention, and our sense of belonging is being met through our children then we will find it very hard not to get sucked in.*

Islay: *The best thing to say to yourself is 'How important is this?' If we have other things in our lives then it's easier not to get sucked in when they are asserting their independence. However, if we have nothing else in our lives to concentrate on, or we make our children the most important thing, everything they then do can become a big issue. There becomes no grading to what they are doing and we end up reacting to everything. The problem with this is it becomes a vicious circle. I feel bad so I'll make you feel bad, you feel bad so you'll make me feel bad. At some point someone needs to break away from the cycle. Your child won't be able to do that so as you are the adult it is your responsibility.*

Paris: *This does make me think. I've a feeling I need to recognise my needs and to look at how I'm getting them met. I think in the past I have tried to get my needs met through Riley and in some ways I probably still am. I do share an awful lot with him. Well it's just that he's usually the only one who's around. I'm wondering whether I have been treating him more like a friend than my child.*

Kim: *That really shows how important it is to recognise that you have needs and that you meet them positively. Taking responsibility for your own well-being is something that we can all do. It makes a huge difference to how effective we are as a parent.*

Anne: *It's strange thinking about this with the big age gaps that I've got. My eldest is 29 and my youngest 8. When I think about my older children I suppose I still try to parent them and tell them what to do, well … it's mainly with Sophie. Maybe that needs to change. Perhaps it's about letting them grow up and not doing everything for them. I know I feel guilty but I'm not even sure why, they are grown-ups after all.*

Darren: *That would be a relief. I've been telling you that for ages.*

Anne: *It's so hard to let go and allow your children to make their own decisions.*

Paris: *So, at what age do we let go of them?*

Islay: *Letting go isn't a sudden process and we will be discussing this in another session. However, in the meantime, it's about thinking about your needs and your child's needs and how you are getting them met. Remember the YouTube clip and how our children will copy our coping strategies. We can make them positive, if we choose to.*

The session has come to an end but before the parents leave Kim asks them to share one thing that they are going to take away and try to focus on during the week.

Angie: *I'm going to think about the scales and the correct balance between giving support and trying to take control.*

Anne: *It's made me think about what need I'm meeting when I try to help everyone, and whether I'm doing too much? I need to think about that.*

Darren: *I think Anne does too much for everyone especially her older children and I keep telling her that.*

Anne: *That also includes you though, Darren.*

Islay: *So, Darren, what one thing are you going to take away?*

Darren: *I don't know.*

Paris: *How about whether you expect Anne to look after you too much too?*

Anne smiles and Darren looks a bit put out but nods his head.

Margaret: *What I'm taking away is 'What would Donkey say?' when I have doubts.*

The group chuckle at the image.

Paris: *It's done my head in. There's so much going on and has made me think about so much that I need time to think about it all.*

Kim: *There's some great awareness that's taken place here today. This week it would be really good to try and notice how you are getting your needs met. It will be a good step to recognise the links between how you are feeling and how you behave.*

Islay: *There is another health warning here. This session may have made you feel that you have a lot of work to do, and that the responsibility is weighing heavy on your shoulders. This is quite a common way to feel at this point. Try not to be hard on yourself, or judge yourself for what you haven't done yet. Take some comfort from the knowledge that your awareness has been increased and that with responsibility comes choice and opportunity. With your increased knowledge and awareness you have the opportunity to make some changes to your behaviour if you choose to do so.*

The parents have been given a lot of information in this session. As they leave the room some of them, as Islay predicted, are carrying the responsibility heavily on their shoulders. Martin was in good spirits. It had been a good session for him and some things were starting to make sense. He had come to the group feeling that he was a rubbish parent; it was hard to talk in a group as it reminded him of school. At this session he had started to talk more, he wasn't so afraid of getting it wrong. When he was talking about the fun times they had at home it had made him realise that there was a lot of good going on. Martin left the room thinking that there was light at the end of the tunnel, at last.

Margaret was slow to move out of her chair as she let the others rush past her. It wasn't the weight of responsibility on her shoulders it was the heaviness of the fear in her stomach that was holding her back. She was used to responsibility. Margaret wasn't sure what the fear was about but there had been a lot in this session that had made her think. Everything had jumbled up together, stuff from the past, her situation now with Damien, and how useless she felt. It was too much really. As she left the room Margaret wondered whether the 'Donkey' word would work; she hoped so as she didn't want to let the group down.

**Take the time to treat yourself to a nice warm bubble bath. It can have an instant calming effect.**

 ## FOR REFLECTION

1. How are you meeting your need for independence (self-sufficiency)?
2. How are you meeting your need for control (autonomy)?
3. How are you meeting your need to belong (fitting in)?
4. How are you meeting your need for fun and enjoyment?
5. Go back over the questions and apply them to your child. How do they get these needs met?
6. What have you learned in this chapter that will help you to behave differently when your child is being violent?

# 5

# CLIMB A MOUNTAIN

 **Praise is magic.** Give positive feedback to your child by noticing the positive and praising them.

A few days after Session 4, Islay and Kim phoned the parents to find out how they were getting on. They got a mixed response.

When the group returns it is obvious that Darren and Anne are struggling.

Margaret: *I've been longing to come back. I went home and told Damien about 'Donkey' and he was laughing. Now we say it to each other. If either of us is feeling down or anxious we say 'What would Donkey say?' we both then start to laugh. We've not had so many arguments. I still get worried if Damien is late for school but now I just say 'I don't think Donkey will be happy with that'. He then gets a move on. It's really strange how much it's helped to distract us both from our anxiety.*

Paris: *Wow, well done you. I've been pretty quiet. Riley kept asking me if I was okay. That in itself is a small miracle; he doesn't usually care how I feel. I did say to him that I didn't think he cared and he looked surprised and said, 'Of course I care, you're my mum aren't you?' It did make me wonder about all those times I thought he was* doing all this stuff to upset me. I'm beginning to wonder if it actually has nothing to do with me. I'm starting to think more about how I see things. Maybe I take things too personally.

Anne: Darren seems fed up with me and Mikki's behaviour is getting worse. Even Peter who keeps telling me to get stronger has started having a go at me.

Darren shifts in his seat and looks uncomfortable.

Angie: What is it you're doing differently Anne?

Anne: After last week I decided I needed to be stronger. I understood how I was trying to keep everyone happy and that I was failing miserably. I realised that as soon as someone asked me to do something I would rush to do it. I decided I'd try a small change to start with so I chose the washing. I told everyone that from now on they needed to put their washing in the wash basket. I was so used to going into their rooms and seeing all of their stuff on the floor. It would make me so cross. It's that sort of thing that starts most of our arguments. It's been really hard because I like such a clean house and not going into their bedrooms has taken all my willpower. But I've done it. They all started moaning at me. Yes, you too, Darren ....

Darren had made a noise but Anne wasn't going to let him interrupt.

Anne: Where's my shirt? Why haven't I got any clean underpants? I was really pleased with myself that I managed to stay calm. I had explained to them all but I know none of them thought I would carry it out. I just kept the bedroom doors closed so that it didn't get to me. It's been harder with you, Darren, because I expected you to support me and you know how I hate an untidy bedroom. It felt like you were doing it to spite me.

Darren stayed quiet as he realised that nothing he could say at that moment would be right. However, Angie had other ideas.

Angie: *Darren, do you not support Anne in trying to get the children to be more responsible?*

Darren: *Well, yes, of course I do but I work long hours and I know you're all going to have a go at me but I just felt Anne was putting me into the same bracket as the children. Treating me like a child.*

Anne was feeling angry and as she lowered her head she muttered under her breath, *'Well, if the shoe fits ….'*

Islay: *It's always difficult when things change as it affects everyone. Darren and Anne, it sounds as if change is happening. The change in itself is good but you're not bringing everyone along with you. Looking back Anne is there anything you could have done to get a different outcome?*

Anne: *I guess I could have explained first to Darren and asked him to support me. I just assumed that he would support me as he doesn't like all the arguments either. He's always saying I shouldn't do so much for the children. I hadn't realised that he expects me to continue to do everything for him.*

Darren: *Yes, it would have helped if you'd spoken to me first. I do want to support you.*

Angie: *I've spent the week thinking about the scales. It's been really useful. When things have happened I've noticed how I interpreted it, and whether it is positive or negative. I've been thinking about what I say to people, especially Harry and how he's hearing it. It's similar I think to what Anne and Darren are going through, it sounds as if at the moment the scales are tipped more towards the negative for both of them. I think it's hard to turn the negative into positive but it's worth making the effort.*

Martin: *How did you get on with geocaching, Angie?*

Angie: *It was so much fun. I took some photos of Philip and Harry holding up the cache. They were so funny sneaking around making sure that no one knew what they were doing. We had taken a picnic and afterwards we sat and ate it in the sunshine. It'll be one of those memories that I will cherish. Thank you, Martin, it was a great thing to do and Philip said to say thank you as well because he enjoyed it so much.*

Kim: *Someone once said 'Don't give your children good habits; give them good memories, because then the good habits will follow'. It sounds as if that is what happened here Angie.*

Anne looks pensive as she takes in what Angie has just said about the positive and negative scales. She had a lot to think about. Darren was also coming to the conclusion that he needed to think about his relationship with Anne. There was no doubt that Anne was changing and he needed to work out whether he was okay with that. Then there's Mikki. He really loves her and wants what's best for her.

 **Say thank you.** Be respectful towards your child, by saying please and thank you and they will learn to be respectful towards you.

Islay: *Last week we looked at how we get our needs met and that all behaviour is meeting a need whether positively or negatively. If it's positive then you are more likely to be able to reach your full potential in life. That doesn't mean that everything will go right for*

*you all of the time. It means that when things do go wrong you will have a greater resilience and will be able to get things into perspective. However if your needs are being met in negative ways then your resilience will be low. It means that when things go wrong you are less likely to be able to recover from it quickly.*

Margaret: *I know what that feels like. Something goes wrong and it's a bit like the circus act where the person is spinning loads of plates on sticks and they're working really hard to keep them spinning. I feel just like that person. When one plate falls I give up and then all the plates fall and I end up feeling miserable.*

Kim: *Do you think sometimes you are working hard keeping other people's plates spinning? Might it be okay to drop those plates that don't belong to you?*

Anne: *Wow that's me. One of my plates was collecting everyone's washing and I guess I am letting that one fall.*

Kim: *I'd like you to get back into your pairs again. Here's some paper – can you draw the plates that you are spinning? Name the plates to show what the tasks are. Then look at the ones that you could let go of or hand back to the person they belong to. Remember that it needs to be age appropriate. There will be things you need to do for a three-year-old but you shouldn't be doing them for an eight-year-old or a twenty-eight-year-old.*

They get into their pairs. They start to draw the plates and add words like, 'the washing', 'tidying their rooms', 'not taking their PE kit into school when they've forgotten it', 'clearing up after the whole family'. Islay and Kim are pleased that the parents are really beginning to recognise what things they might be able to let go.

Islay: *That exercise will have given you some idea of the tasks you need to keep hold of and those you could let go. We are going to be covering this in another session in more detail, but it's really important to start thinking about what small changes you might be able to make now which will help your children be more responsible for themselves.*

Anne: *Let's not forget partners.*

Islay: *In this session we are reintroducing the panic zone from comfort, stretch, panic, and we are going to look at what happens when we go into our panic zone. Last week we looked at how you get your needs met in SAFER ways, which is meeting them in a positive way. If we mix up the letters of SAFER we can make the word FEARS. This represents the way we get our needs met in a negative way, it is our coping strategies.*

Kim begins to draw a diagram on the flip chart to illustrate what Islay is saying:

| F | E | A | R | S |
|---|---|---|---|---|
| | | **Coping Strategies** | | |

Islay: *Each of us will have different coping strategies. We need to explore what ours might be. When we get our needs met in SAFER ways we are in the part of our brain where we can make sense of what is happening to us and we are able to think through our choices in appropriate ways. However if we go into our panic zone we automatically shift to a different part of our brain. This is based on the Fight or Flight response (Canon 1920). We call it FEARS and it is the opposite of SAFER. FEARS are our automatic coping strategies. We've talked about getting our needs met in negative ways and our habits. This will help you to understand your patterns of behaviour and will give you an* insight into what might be happening in Box 4 of the Window to Self-Knowledge.

The parents are instantly interested. This is the box that seems the most confusing.

Kim: *Can anyone remember what they said it felt like to be in panic?*

Paris: *I get extremely angry. It's like a red mist and I start shouting.*

Margaret: *I go quiet and just want to curl up in a ball. I get so frightened.*

Islay: *It's a horrid place to be and it is exhausting. The problem is that something has happened and it has triggered this response within you. Sometimes it's not about what is actually happening in front of you but it will trigger a memory that makes you scared. Can you think of a piece of music or a particular smell that puts you back into a time in the past?*

Martin: *Music. Every time I hear the song 'My Baby Just Cares for Me' it reminds me of my mum. She used to play it all the time.*

Kim: *Is that a nice memory?*

Martin: *Yes, because she used to dance around the table to it.*

Islay: *Some memories are good and send us back to a happier time, but what do you think would happen if, for example, your child sounds like and looks like a relative who you disapprove of?*

Angie: *Wow, that's like Harry. He's a bit like my brother who ended up in prison. Sometimes the way he looks at me reminds me of the way my brother used to look at my mum. He sounds like him too. I get scared he's going to go the same way.*

Kim: *On those occasions do you think your tone and the consequences you use may be harder because you are treating Harry as if he is your brother?*

Angie: *Thinking about it, I suppose my fear might be making me come down hard on him.*

Kim: *I'm wondering whether Harry understands your concern.*

Angie: *Yes, I tell him that if he's not careful he's going to end up like his uncle.*

Kim: *What message do you think he is getting from that, Angie?*

Margaret: *Oh dear, I do that to Damien too. I guess what he's hearing is that I don't like him. He reminds me of his dad and the times when he used to be violent towards me. Damien knows I can't stand his dad because of what he put us through.*

Islay: *It's normal to feel like that after what you have gone through. However, the important thing to remember is that your children are unique. Yes, they will show us traits that remind us of people within our family, they might even remind us of ourselves, and it's usually the bits we don't like. Our fear will motivate us to try to stop that behaviour in them; we will tend to come down hard on them to stamp it out. Of course your child has no idea about this and will be experiencing something different.*

Angie: *So I may be overreacting to Harry because I am worried that he will turn out like my brother?*

Kim: *Yes it could be. Harry may feel you are being too harsh, as in his eyes he has just got something small wrong and you have overreacted to it. He may then end up thinking you are being unfair.*

Islay: *This can also happen when you expect too much from your child. If your child gets something wrong and you make them feel stupid, they may give up trying. This will breed anger as you are both reacting from a negative place.*

Islay: *The more we understand our triggers and then our reactions to those triggers then the smaller Box 4 will become.*

Islay refers back to the diagram that Kim had drawn.

Islay: *In the same way that we used SAFER to illustrate how our needs are met positively, FEARS represents how our needs are met negatively. This is when we go into our panic state and we stop being able to process the information we are getting. Basically we stop thinking and making sense of what is happening and we just react.*

Paris: *I was crossing the road the other day and a motorbike appeared out of nowhere, I had to jump out of the way. If I hadn't it would have hit me. I didn't have time to think I just reacted. Do you mean like that?*

Islay: *Yes. That was an appropriate way for you to deal with that threat. However our experiences may make something a threat, which isn't an actual threat.*

Margaret: *Oh, is that like with Damien and me. He says something which sounds like his dad. At that point I get frightened and I stop seeing Damien for who he is and I react as if he was his dad.*

Kim: *Yes, exactly. Our memories take over and we react rather than respond. The thinking part of our brain shuts down and we go into instinctive survival.*

Kim adds the following words to the FEARS diagram that she had started earlier:

F stands for Freeze
E stands for Excrete
A stands for Aggression
R stands for Running away
S stands for Self-abuse

The group looks at the words and there is some confusion on their faces.

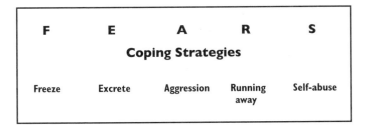

| **F** | **E** | **A** | **R** | **S** |
|-------|-------|-------|-------|-------|
| | | **Coping Strategies** | | |
| Freeze | Excrete | Aggression | Running away | Self-abuse |

Islay: *Looking at the word* **Freeze** *what does it make you think of?*

Margaret: *I think of me. I get almost paralysed. If I get really scared I can have a panic attack. I can't move and I think I'm dying. It's horrible. I was taught that as long as I breathe slowly I start to calm down but at the time it's so awful. I used to get a lot of them but they are getting better. It really scares Damien. But then he gets so angry with me especially if it's after he's done something and my worry takes over. I guess it's when I'm scared and he's hit me, like his dad did. Thinking about it although he gets angry it does stop him from hitting me. I suppose it might scare him too.*

Kim: *It can also link to when people are depressed. Being stuck is another way of putting it.*

Martin: *There are times when I feel so stuck, like nothing is ever going to change. That's depressing.*

Islay: *The difficulty is that our memories tell us that this isn't going to work and then surprise, surprise it doesn't. We can't change our memories but we can stop them from controlling us.*

Kim: *What about the word* **Excrete***?*

The group laughs, wondering where on earth the conversation is going.

Anne: *Well I think of poo! And not Winnie-the-Pooh either!*

Islay: *You are right. Have you heard the saying 'I was so scared I shit myself?'*

Everyone nods.

Islay: *When we are in extreme fear the body's response is to try and survive. That means all of your energy has to go to keeping you alive. That's where the adrenaline comes from; it needs to give you enough power to escape whatever the threat may be. All the parts of the body that aren't necessary for your survival will temporarily shut down. The body doesn't need to waste energy on them. That includes the muscles that control the bladder and bowel. It's unpleasant, but you are not going to die if you wet or soil yourself.*

Darren: *I've never thought of it like that. My dad was very controlling and I'm sorry to say I wet the bed until I was fifteen. It was awful. When I was eight my mum took me to the doctor and I was checked out. I think she was fed up of washing the sheets the whole time. They told her to stop giving me drinks after 6pm and to wake me up. They thought I was a very deep sleeper so I just didn't wake up to go to the loo. I'm not convinced. When I was fifteen my dad left home so I'm wondering whether all that was happening because I was so scared of him.*

Anne looks really taken aback. She never knew that about Darren. She's starting to wonder whether that has something to do with him needing to be in control. Was it that he was copying his dad or was it the fear of being out of control that would trigger those negative feelings? Perhaps he was afraid he'd start to wet the bed again. Who knows? Anne is beginning to realise that she needs to feel she has some control as well.

Kim: *Thank you Darren for sharing. It must have been difficult for you growing up.*

Darren: *Yes. I never wanted to be invited for a sleepover and if I was I'd make sure I'd stay awake all night. I remember feeling angry all the time as to why this was happening to me. It was just so embarrassing. My dad used to mock me, which just made it worse.*

Islay: *The next word is* **Aggression**. *Has anyone got any ideas about this one?*

Paris: *That sounds like me ... Miss Angry they used to call me. I would hit and I'd scream and shout.*

Islay: *There are two ways of showing aggression, Paris, and you've have just mentioned both of them, they are by being verbally and physically aggressive. Can anyone tell me what happens to their speech when they get really angry?*

Paris: *I get very loud, and I can't find the right word and I swear a lot.*

Kim: *That's exactly what happens. We can't fully access the part of our brain that controls our words. We're not able to use our thinking brain, so we haven't got the full use of our vocabulary. The chances are that we will end up reacting emotionally and we'll say things that we later regret.*

Paris: *That's definitely me, I'm forever doing that. If I'm on a night out and I've been drinking I can get really nasty. I always have to go back and apologise to everyone. I don't mean to, it's like I can't help it.*

Islay: *We are going to encourage you to stop saying 'I can't help it' and to start looking at what you can change. The difficulty with alcohol is that it reduces your social skills and allows your anger to motivate you. Paris, uncovering Box 4 for you might be by looking at your anger. Maybe it goes something like this: I find it hard to be assertive so I need an excuse to tell people I'm angry with them. When I go on a night out I can justify drinking lots of alcohol; that's my excuse to get angry and tell people what I really think of them. I can then blame the alcohol and say 'Oh that was just the alcohol talking, not me'.*

Paris looks a bit surprised; she feels as if Islay is being judgmental.

Martin: *I think you've just described me. That's what I do, I justify it by saying I need time out from the kids.*

Kim: *You do need time out and it's really important to work out whether you are doing it in a positive way or a negative way. It's essential when building healthy relationships to find a way of being able to say how you feel in a manner that people will hear and understand. It's about taking responsibility for how you feel. We will be looking at communication in a later session which hopefully will help.*

Paris: *I'm going to look forward to that. I'm glad it's not just me who behaves like this.*

She looks at Martin gratefully

Islay: *The challenge is always to make sense of why we behave in the way we do and what is motivating us. It's also hard when we hear people saying things to us that we find difficult. We have a choice of listening, hearing and working out whether what that person is saying is correct, or we can get defensive. It helps you to stay in control. I am not judging you, Paris. I am giving you a possible reason. It is up to you to say whether I am correct or not. After all, you know yourself far better than I know you.*

Paris looks a bit happier and the other members of the group are beginning to make sense of what they are hearing. They now understand that it is their choice to hear or disregard the feedback that they receive. They realise that if they are serious about wanting things to change for the better then they need to keep an open mind.

Kim: *The next word is* **Running away**. *What do you think this means?*

Paris: *Is that a bit like I did when I jumped out of the way of the motorbike?*

Kim: *Yes. We run away or hide from situations. Has anyone had a bill come through the door that they have put in a drawer and not opened?*

Most of the parents groan and identify with this.

Martin: *I've got a whole drawer full of them.*

Margaret: *I did that. I didn't have any money to pay bills so I did the ostrich thing and pretended it wasn't happening. It got so bad that the bailiffs were banging on the door. It was an awful time for me. I hid behind the sofa and made Damien keep quiet. They eventually went away, but I was terrified that they were going to come back. My friend told me that I could get help at the local church and they put me in touch with a debt agency. It was such a relief to get good advice.*

Kim: *It's a lot to cope with when you are on your own and parents don't always know that there are agencies that can help. Sometimes you have to be brave enough to admit you need help. It doesn't mean you are a failure, it just means you need help at this moment. Has anyone needed help in the past, but doesn't need it now?*

Angie: *I went through a really difficult time. I got into a lot of debt when Philip was out of work. He's now got a good job and so things are better, but at the time the hardest thing was going for help. It hit his pride and he felt he'd failed as a husband and a father. He got really depressed about it.*

Islay: *This links back to our resilience and our view of ourselves as being people with all the answers. When we haven't got all the answers we sometimes associate this with failure. Life can throw some awful situations at us. If we think about children being bullied at school, some cope and some don't. Has anyone got any idea why?*

Angie: *Is that about how confident you are?*

Kim: *Yes it is, but it's not the outward confidence, it is the inner confidence where you know that you are an okay person.*

Anne: *That's like my Thomas. He's the most beautiful person out. He just has this quiet confidence. He doesn't brag and he accepts who he is. He just seems at peace with himself. He was bullied at school because he's gay but it never used to faze him. He would just smile and tell them they were only jealous. That would make people embarrassed and in the end they stopped. They realised that they weren't going to get a reaction out of him. He always had loads of girls to go around with and they all loved him.*

Islay: *The last word is* **Self-abuse***. Has anyone any idea what this might link to?*

Paris: *Is that self-harm?*

Islay: *In a way, yes; it's about the different forms of self-abuse that people use and it is a way of coping with emotional pain. What sort of things can you think of that you might do to yourself if you were trying to stop the hurting inside?*

Margaret: *I used to self-harm. I hated myself and would feel awful and somehow I found the cutting stopped those feelings for a while.*

Martin: *Didn't it hurt you?*

Margaret: *No, I never felt the physical pain; it helped to stop the emotional pain inside for a while.*

Anne: *Sophie used to self-harm and I was always scared that she was trying to kill herself.*

Margaret: *When I cut myself it was never about trying to kill myself. I didn't want to end my life. It was a coping strategy.*

Islay: *It's not immediately easy to see why anyone would intentionally cut themselves, but it is a coping strategy. What we can do is try to find other coping strategies to deal with the feelings that have prompted the self-harming.*

Margaret: *There are other forms of self-harm though, aren't there?*

Kim: *Yes. Can anyone think what they might be?*

Martin: *Well, I've already mentioned alcohol, and I guess it would be drugs too.*

Islay: *As we have already seen it is a fundamental need that we have some control in our lives. When we are feeling out of control the one thing we can control is what we do or don't do to ourselves.*

Margaret: *I was sexually abused when I was little. I always blamed myself and so I ate and ate. That's why I'm so big now. I've tried to lose weight, but as soon as I feel down I go to the fridge.*

Islay: *It is really hard to make sense of why anyone would abuse a child. It is just so wrong. But as children we all have to make sense of what is happening to us. An abuser will be meeting a child's needs but highly negatively. This is hard to understand but as we have already discussed our needs will be met one way or another. Think about what it was like for you as a child. How much control did you have over how you got your needs met?*

You could hear a pin drop in the room. Some of the parents were looking at the floor. This was a really uncomfortable subject for them. Others just looked horrified.

Paris: *Not at all. I had no control. I just had to put up with whatever happened until I was old enough to escape. Riley was my way out.*

Islay: *So now think about you as a child and how you got your needs met but in a negative way.*

Margaret: *The person who abused me lived next door and my mum trusted him. He was always popping in and she'd leave me with him. It was awful. He used to tell me how beautiful I was and that it was our little secret. It was so horrid. It really screwed my head up. I remember part of me wanting to go there because in a funny way he gave me attention and no one else did.*

Kim: *Thank you Margaret for sharing that. Your reaction to the attention was perfectly normal, after all attention is a fundamental need and as a child you will get it where you can. The responsibility wasn't yours it was his.*

Margaret: *I know that now, but sometimes it still gives me doubts as to why he picked me. Did I do something that gave him the wrong message?*

Islay: *The problem is that an abuser will try to pass over the responsibility to the child with words like you have described: 'You're so beautiful, I can't resist you'; 'It'll be our little secret'; 'I'll look after you'. Eventually for survival as a child you have to go along with it. What other choice do you have? However, your behaviour will have changed. It is up to the other adults in your life to recognise that.*

Margaret: *That's exactly what Damien's dad did to me, especially after he hit me. He'd apologise and bring me flowers and promise he'd never do it again. He'd say wear this skirt because it'll hide your knees and you don't want to be giving people the wrong impression. Thinking about it now it's like he knew what to say to control me.*

Kim: *It's very complicated because if we have had that experience our memories will tell us how we should get our needs met. That then becomes our habits.*

Darren: *It's beginning to make sense to me. My father was very controlling and I thought that is how a man should behave, even though I didn't like it. I've justified it in my head that it's okay to be like that because it didn't do me any harm.*

Islay: *This is often a really tricky session as we uncover some of the nastier sides to human behaviour. I believe that fundamentally people are good beings. They are not born horrid. It is the experiences that they have had that will make them horrid. We have an opportunity in thinking about the Window to Self-Knowledge to understand our behaviour and what might be behind it. This will give you the choice of whether you will continue to behave in the same way or choose to do something different which will change the outcome for you and your children.*

Kim: *Take a look at the FEARS diagram that I started earlier and let's see what it looks like when we're getting our needs met in negative ways.*

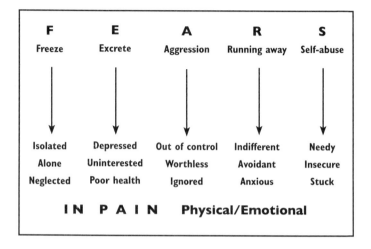

Angie: *If you feel some of these feelings is it a clue that your needs are being met in a negative way?*

Martin: *I've noticed that at the bottom it says IN PAIN physical/ emotional what does that mean?*

Anne: *It makes sense to me, when my first husband died I went through all of those feelings on there. Then I started to ache everywhere on my body, I had headaches and stomach aches. My GP told me that it was most likely linked to bereavement and what I was going through. It was probably because I was so tense. He suggested that I learnt to relax so I started going to yoga, it was fantastic and really helped.*

Kim: *Anne, that is a great link to the physical and emotional pain that we can go through. Yoga is a good way to help relax our bodies.*

Islay: *Once we have worked out why we behave the way we do then we have a chance to change it. The first thing we need to do is to notice our behaviour. Once we become aware of how it is impacting on our children and on us we then have choices.*

Kim: *This has been a tough session and may have left you remembering a difficult past, which you have tried to forget. This isn't about opening wounds, but about acknowledging what has happened.*

Islay: *What has happened to us in the past, good and bad has made us the people we are today. It will have brought out strengths and qualities in you that otherwise may have remained dormant. We can't change the past but we can recognise when the feelings rooted there, spill out and affect us today*

Kim: *Is anyone willing to share what they're taking away from this session?*

Anne: *I am taking away the image of the spinning plates. This session has really helped me realise how much I do and that most of it is for everyone else. It's no wonder that I am so tired. The FEARS were good too; it helped me make some sense of the past.*

Darren: *Talking about my childhood and how my dad was towards me. That's been tough but at least I'm not like that with Mikki. It's confirmed that I'm not like him, though, so that's what I'm taking away.*

Paris: *What you said about alcohol and it being an excuse for bad behaviour. I thought you were having a go at me but I can see that it's about Box 4. I didn't like hearing it, but I needed to.*

Margaret: *The FEARS made sense to me; I seem to use all of them. Well, all except the aggression one, it's hard for me to get angry. I* need to remember to keep using the word 'Donkey'; it worked well for us.

Angie: *I'm taking away 'You can't change your memories, but you can stop them controlling you'. I have had a lightbulb moment too: I need to stop talking to Harry as if he is my brother; what my brother did has nothing to do with Harry.*

The group remained quiet for a moment while they absorbed what had been said. As they began to leave the room some of the parents reflected on the session and some wondered what they were going home to. Angie was so glad that she had persevered with the group and not gone with her first impressions. At first it didn't feel like it was her type of group at all, most of the parents seemed unhappy and worn out. She had been worried that they might pull her down with them. She had found her place in the group now and the others seemed to be accepting her suggestions and her feedback. They all seemed a bit happier too. She had held her breath a bit when she had asked Darren whether he supported Anne, but he didn't seem to mind. She wouldn't have normally said something like that. Angie laughed to herself as she noted the subtle changes that she was making to her behaviour.

Paris was feeling quite proud of herself as she picked up her coat and headed towards the door. There was a time when she would have stormed out of the room if anyone had questioned her behaviour as Islay had done in this session. Her first thought was 'Who does she think she is!'; but now she was glad that she hadn't given in to her first reaction. When she calmed herself down she understood that Islay was helping her to discover what was in Box 4, not simply having a go at her. What had interested Paris was that Islay said that she had a choice, to listen or not to listen; it made it easier to accept. Paris wondered whether she could try that out with Riley, his aggression seemed to be getting more and more out of control. She wanted to talk to him about it but he was just like her and would storm off the minute she mentioned it.

 **Rather than beat yourself up for making a mistake, reflect on what you have learned. It's not the falling over that matters, it's the getting up.**

#  FOR REFLECTION

1. What are the sorts of things you do when you are in the panic zone? Of the FEARS states which one are you likely to use?

    Freeze?

    Excrete?

    Aggression?

    Running away?

    Self-abuse?

2. What happens to your behaviour when you are in panic?

3. How do you respond to your child when you are in panic?

# 6

# STRIKE A BALANCE

 **Give melting moments.** An unexpected gift or treat shows that you are thinking about your child and lets them know that they are valued. It doesn't need to be expensive: it could just be their favourite food or drink. It gives them that warm feeling, the melting factor.

During the week, Kim and Islay phoned the parents to see how their week was going. It had been a tough session the previous week and it had brought back some uncomfortable memories; memories that had been locked away, because remembering would be too painful. The phone calls revealed that some of the parents were beginning to recognise that it was okay to remember. Remembering helped them to understand their triggers and detach from the emotions. Keeping their past hidden meant that old hurts and anger were likely to leak out and affect other areas of their lives.

Anne and Darren were on their own separate journeys. Anne was growing stronger and Darren was starting the journey of remembering. Darren had been thinking more about his childhood and was trying to understand it from his perspective now as an adult. He realised that when he was emotionally triggered he usually ended up blaming himself. He was beginning to think that maybe everything wasn't always his entire fault, and that some of the memories may need correcting. He realised that he might need help with this.

The group assembled for another session. Most of them were wondering whether this session would be as tough as the last one.

Kim: *I know that the last session was hard and that some of you have struggled this week. How have you got on?*

Darren: *I started to realise that I'm like my dad and that scared me. I realise that I need to stop looking back as a child and look back as an adult. I know that seems odd but each time I remember my dad I feel so angry and it's like I'm back there as his child and he's controlling me. I seem to forget I'm an adult now.*

Islay: *That's quite a step to have taken. How has it been at home?*

Anne: *I've been really thinking about things. Sophie rang and expected me to go and look after the children. I love seeing my grandchildren but I realised the way she asked me wasn't very nice and it got me to thinking that I've actually put up with a lot of disrespect from my children and I am worth talking to nicely.*

Margaret: *I found it really hard last week, especially sharing with you what happened to me growing up. Darren, what you have just said about looking at the memories but with an adult take on things has made so much sense to me. Last week I was remembering, but now I think – like you – I was getting stuck remembering it all as a child, as if it was still happening. It hasn't been a good week and I'm surprised I even came tonight.*

There's a murmur of support around the room telling Margaret how glad they are that she has come back.

Margaret: *Damien on the other hand has been really good, really helpful. I suspect he was scared. The last time I started to feel like this I took an overdose and ended up in hospital.*

Kim: *How are you feeling now?*

Margaret: *I'm okay. I did remember what you'd said about our children worrying about us so I was able to reassure Damien. I didn't feel like killing myself, it was actually good to be able to talk about it. I've been feeling upset and sad all week.*

Islay: *It's good to feel sad because it's the start of grieving for the past.*

Martin: *I've always thought you can't change the past, so there's no point looking at it. I've realised now that I need to. I agree with what Darren has said. I'm also wondering if this is something I can do myself, or whether I need to get help.*

Kim: *Looking at our past is a really brave step to take and sometimes we do need help to make sense of our memories. When we are used to people seeing us and responding to us as a victim then it can be hard to move away from that to being victorious.*

Margaret: *I like the thought of being victorious. I'm going to remember that, a bit like saying 'Donkey' when I'm feeling miserable I'm going to remember I can be victorious and try to find a solution to make that happen.*

Margaret is smiling. She loves these images and it helps to keep her focused.

Paris: *All this week I've been watching myself, looking at how I behave and it has been weird. I went out Saturday night and had a* few drinks and then caught myself getting irritated. I realised that if I had kept drinking I would probably snap. My mates were amazed as I said I'm off home now. They tried to stop me going home but I knew if I stayed they'd buy me more drinks and I wouldn't be able to say no. It felt odd going home early.

Angie: *What time was that then?*

Paris: *Two in the morning.*

Angie: *You call that early? I'd be dead on my feet at that time. I guess that's the difference in our ages. Paris, I was wondering, what is it you like doing?*

Paris: *Well, I would have said going out with my mates before, but I'm not sure now. I was always good at knitting … I know, don't laugh, but I used to make all sorts of things. I loved it.*

Angie: *I belong to a knitting group that meets every Wednesday morning in a coffee shop and we chat and talk about what we are knitting. I get loads of wool and a lot of my needles from charity shops. Why don't you come along?*

Paris looks absolutely thrilled that Angie has invited her and readily agrees that she would like that.

Angie: *A bit like you Paris I was watching myself this week. Last Tuesday when Harry came in from school he was in such a foul mood. I would normally react to him but this time I didn't and eventually he took himself off to his room. After a while I shouted upstairs and asked if he wanted a drink. He came straight down and he started to talk to me in a much calmer way. Philip was very impressed with how I handled the situation differently.*

**Find three things you have in common.** Have a conversation about the things you both like, and the activities you can do together. Find at least three common interests.

Kim: *We have already talked about how our behaviour is affected by internal and external factors. This week we are going to look even deeper into our own behaviour. This will include how we communicate with our children, how we meet their needs, and how we discipline them. We will also be thinking about what our children may be experiencing from our behaviour.*

Islay: *To make sense of this, can you think about how you behave towards your child when you are stressed. That will give you a true picture of what your child may be experiencing. What sort of thing makes you stressed and how might this cause your behaviour to change towards your child?*

Paris: *With me, it's when I get a call from the school.*

Margaret: *When I haven't any money and Damien demands new expensive trainers.*

Angie: *When I'm expected to go out for a business function with Philip and Harry is playing up.*

Martin: *When the kids won't get up in the morning and get ready for school.*

Islay: *Thank you, some great examples of how stress affects you. As I mentioned, the way that you behave towards your child as a parent can be affected by internal factors such as how you are feeling, which one of your children you are parenting and* which developmental stage your child is going through. It is also affected by external factors such as financial constraints, the breakdown of relationships, and bereavement.

Paris: Is that like when I go out for the night and the next morning I'm hung over and I get really wound up if Riley then refuses to get up? Actually, thinking about it, he does really play up on those mornings. It's like he knows I haven't got the energy to cope with him.

Kim: Yes, you have just described the two factors. External because you went out and drank too much, and the internal because you are tired and hungover. It's okay to go out, but you need to remember the impact on your child.

Paris: Oh no, I think I have taken it out on Riley in the past and I guess he must have got angry thinking why are you blaming me for your tiredness and headache. I know I've said to him, 'You're giving me a headache' when it wasn't him at all, it was too much booze.

Angie: I think you've just increased your Box 1, Paris.

Everyone agrees and Paris smiles.

Kim: We have devised the following questionnaire, which will help you to identify your strengths as a parent. Take some time to complete this now and be as honest with yourself as you can. If you have more than one child please focus on the one you are struggling with at the moment.

| | Seldom | Some-times | Often |
|---|---|---|---|
| **Warmth** | | | |
| 1. I consider my child's feelings in any situation | | | |
| 2. I allow my child to express their feelings | | | |
| 3. My actions tell my child I love them | | | |
| 4. I have fun with my child | | | |
| 5. I like my child | | | |
| 6. I give my child positive messages | | | |
| 7. I say 'thank you' to my child | | | |
| 8. I praise my child | | | |
| | | | |
| **Firm** | | | |
| 1. I set clear rules, boundaries | | | |
| 2. I set appropriate consequences | | | |
| 3. I am consistent in my approach | | | |
| 4. I am able to say 'No' to my child | | | |
| 5. I am able to take control when necessary | | | |
| 6. My words and actions give the same message to my child | | | |
| 7. My children believe that I will do as I say | | | |
| 8. I have routines and can be flexible when required | | | |

# STRIKE A BALANCE

| | Seldom | Some-times | Often |
|---|---|---|---|
| **Fair** | | | |
| 1. I notice what my child does right every day | | | |
| 2. I listen to my child | | | |
| 3. I see things from my child's perspective | | | |
| 4. I allow my child to have choices | | | |
| 5. I recognise that my child has their own thoughts and feelings | | | |
| 6. I allow my child to make mistakes | | | |
| 7. I say sorry to my child when I have got it wrong | | | |
| 8. I support and encourage my child | | | |
| **As your child grows up;** | | | |
| 1. I am willing to discuss matters with my child | | | |
| 2. I am able to negotiate with my child | | | |
| 3. I encourage my child to become independent | | | |
| 4. I teach my child about rights and responsibilities for themselves and others | | | |

|  | Seldom | Some-times | Often |
|---|---|---|---|
| 5. I value my child's views and opinions |  |  |  |
| 6. I am interested in my child's goals |  |  |  |
| 7. I monitor my child's use of technology |  |  |  |
| 8. I provide a healthy diet |  |  |  |
| **Looking after yourself as a parent** |  |  |  |
| 1. I have fun in my life |  |  |  |
| 2. I spend time with my friends |  |  |  |
| 3. My family are supportive of me |  |  |  |
| 4. I exercise regularly |  |  |  |
| 5. I like learning new things |  |  |  |
| 6. I take the opportunity to be creative |  |  |  |
| 7. I am aware of my own feelings |  |  |  |
| 8. I spend time alone without distractions |  |  |  |

When it is clear that the parents have completed the questionnaire Kim asks them to add up their score. Then she begins to explain what the scoring means.

Kim: *All of the questions relate to a positive quality associated with parenting. You have now identified what you are doing well. Any of the ones that you have marked as 'Often' are your* strengths. Any of the ones that you have marked as 'Sometimes' will help you to see that you are on the right track. Any of the ones that you have marked as 'Seldom' are the areas that you need to work on.

Islay: *You can take this one step further by recording the total number of ticks that you have in the 'Often' column in the table below;*

| | Total (Often) |
|---|---|
| **Warmth** | |
| **Firm** | |
| **Fair** | |
| **As your child grows up** | |
| **Looking after yourself as a parent** | |

Islay: *The higher numbers on this chart will show you where you are putting the most energy. For example you may be concentrating on the 'warmth' more than anything else or on 'firm' rather than anything else. Is anyone willing to share what they have discovered?*

Margaret: *No surprise here, mine is high on the warmth, but low everywhere else, and especially low on the 'Looking after yourself as a parent'.*

Paris: *Well mine shows high on firm and looking after myself, so I guess no surprises there either.*

Angie: *I've changed since coming to this group. If I had filled this form in two months ago I would have scored much higher on firm. I was so worried that Harry was going to end up like my brother that I was coming down really hard on him. I thought that I could stop him behaving like my brother but it was making him rebel so he was ending up like him anyway. I've backed off since coming here and his behaviour has improved. There is still a way to go but I am feeling more confident that I can handle anything Harry does.*

.

Darren: *My highest by a long way is warmth. It shows I really love Mikki.*

Islay: *Now that you have identified where your focus lies it is important to work out what your child may be experiencing from you. For example, you may think that you are showing your child love, yet if it is to the extreme then their experience could be feeling smothered. You may think you are being firm with your child, yet if it is to the extreme your child could be feeling controlled. You may think that you are being fair with your child but if it is to the extreme your child could be feeling that they are in control of the relationship.*

Margaret: *I've just realised what it must feel like for Damien when I try to do everything for him. He may think I don't trust him to do it for himself.*

Islay: *Yes, Margaret, that links back to the messages that we give our children. If someone is giving you the message that you can't do things for yourself eventually you are going to stop trying. Ultimately it will make you angry.*

Anne: *I think I am so stressed all of the time that I haven't really thought about how Mikki feels. I just get so annoyed with her. If she would just do what I asked her to do I would be happy.*

Islay: *This is what happens when your needs as a parent aren't being met in appropriate ways, you will get them met through your children. It suddenly becomes their responsibility to try and make you happy.*

Anne: *So you're saying it isn't their responsibility to make me feel good. I have to find that in other ways.*

Paris: *Riley doesn't make me feel good. He's forever telling me he hates me. However, I do think I'm a bit confusing at times because although I'm hard I do give in to him.*

Kim: *How do you think Riley makes sense of that?*

Paris: *Well the one thing I'm beginning to realise is he is a bright boy. I think he knows me very well and he knows how to get his own way.*

Kim: *It sounds as if it's difficult to work out who is parenting whom. Sometimes it can help if we think of what state we are operating from and how that then affects our child.*

To explain this, Kim uses an adaption of the Transactional Analysis model by Eric Berne (1910–1970). Kim writes the following three words: 'Parent', 'Adult', 'Child'.

Kim: *These are the three states that we can operate from. If we are being a parent to our child then it allows them to be a child. If we are being more like an adult to our child then we may be pushing them to be an adult too quickly. If we're acting like a child to our child then we may be pushing them to behave as a parent and make them feel responsible for the things that we should be responsible for.*

Margaret: *Oh dear, I think I have been like a child with Damien which at times has got him acting like my parent. I do say to him, 'You're not my dad you know'.*

Kim: *What does he do when he behaves like a parent to you?*

Margaret: *Well, when I get scared and anxious, he looks after me,* but then he tells me what to do all the time. He says 'Don't wear that; don't eat that; don't go there'.

Anne: *Isn't that how you described Damien's dad?*

Margaret: *Oh, yes ... I hadn't seen that. I thought because he's not around now it wouldn't be affecting Damien.*

Martin: *That's made me think of that DVD we watched. Do you think he's copied him and thinks this is how you behave with women?*

Margaret: *Well, I suppose so, but I do tell him you need to respect me.*

Islay: *It's so interesting to think about what we say and what our children actually hear. We will be looking at communication next week, but it's good to have identified this Margaret. If you were operating from a parent state instead of a child state what do you think would be different?*

Margaret: *I would feel more in charge. It's difficult to know what to do but maybe the form can help me. I need to get a better balance on my form.*

Margaret picks up her completed form.

Margaret: *Looking at this I should allow him to do more, to be more responsible for himself and be less responsible for me. I also need to look after myself better ... umm I may need some help on that one.*

Paris: *This is making me think. I may have been treating Riley more like an adult. It's like we're best friends. Of course it's difficult now as he's sixteen and he needs to take more responsibility.*

Kim: *Can you think of how you have treated him more like an adult than a child?*

Paris: *Well, this is a bit embarrassing to say but I would tell him about my nights out and what happened. I guess that gave him more information than he needed. Actually thinking about it I wonder if it would make him anxious when I went out. He used to play up terribly.*

Martin: *Ha, I don't have time to think about what state I operate in. It's much harder when you have so many children and they have such different needs.*

Islay: *Yes, you're right Martin; it's easier just to keep doing what you have always done. Taking the time to think about what state you are operating from with each child may help you to make sense of their behaviour.*

Kim: *If you have one child behaving differently in a family, it's worth thinking about whether you treat them differently. It could be that you are expecting them to be older than their years, or becoming exasperated when they get things wrong.*

It's clear that everyone is thinking more about the way they behave and what that means for their children. The session is coming to an end and Islay asks the parents to share one thing that they are taking away to focus on in the coming week.

Anne: *This session has made me realise that I'm afraid of telling the truth to my children. I don't like the way they talk to me but if I say that, or if I say no to something they want me to do, I'm worried that they would hate me.*

Darren: *I've always said that you rush round to Sophie's at the drop of a hat.*

Anne looks fed up.

Islay: *Darren, it's always easier to notice what other people need to change, especially when it's your partner. The trick is to think about what you can do differently irrespective of Anne. Have you thought about anything?*

Darren is unhappy with what he has heard. He feels as if he has been ticked off in front of the whole group. He chooses not to say anything in response but he is beginning to realise that he can't stay the same and that change is coming whether he likes it or not. He has a difficult decision to make. He can either stay in control of this change or he can fight against it. At the moment he is fighting against it. After a bit of an awkward silence Angie speaks up.

Angie: *I think I can understand a little of what Darren may be going through. When Philip lost his job we really started arguing. It was awful. He felt miserable and I got annoyed as I felt he wasn't doing enough to get a job. We nearly split up. I think we both went through the motions of parenting Harry. To be honest there were times when we'd argue about who was going to do his breakfast. As Philip was at home I expected him to do more for Harry and to do more around the house. It must have been awful for Harry. He's always been very close to his dad, he idolises him. In Harry's eyes his dad can't do anything wrong which used to make me even madder. Thinking about it, it was about that time that Harry started being really nasty to me. Not to his dad. I could never understand it as I hadn't changed.*

Margaret: *You say you hadn't changed but maybe you had. You had Philip home all day and he wasn't doing what you expected him to do.*

Angie: *Well, yes. I'd changed towards Philip but not towards Harry.*

Margaret: *Harry would have picked up on how you were, just like*

*Damien does. He wouldn't have liked you getting at his dad. Even though Damien saw his dad hitting me, he sort of made excuses for him. I was confused as to why he would want to see him when he'd been so nasty. I remember saying to him 'Why do you want to see him?' One day he said to me, 'Well, he didn't hit me and he used to take me out and do nice things with me.' I was shocked; I couldn't believe that he would think like that.*

Paris: *We don't know what they're thinking do we?*

Margaret: *Well, once he got started he followed on by saying, 'You probably deserved to be hit the way you nagged him. It's all down to you that I don't see him any more'.*

Paris: *That's a horrible thing for him to say to you.*

Margaret: *Well, to a certain extent he's right. I had him arrested and then he left us. Damien had no choice over that, and he wasn't all bad. He did take Damien out but he had a drug problem so he wasn't reliable and used to let Damien down. Then I started to drink so that I could sleep at night, otherwise I'd lie in bed and worry. It was an awful time. I guess the drinking became my coping strategy.*

Martin: *A drink at night to help you sleep isn't bad.*

Islay: *As with everything, it's about balance. Paris, what about you?*

Paris: *I thought you'd forget about me .... It's been a bit tough as I'm realising that I had Riley so I could escape home, and I wanted someone to make me feel good and to love me, and now I've used him like a best friend. I've told him everything. He's always there when I need someone. I realise now that is wrong but I've no idea what to do about it. When he gets angry he is so threatening and he has hit me. I've got all this information now and I just feel I've really failed him and I've been such a bad mother.*

107

The group start to make noises about her not being a bad mother, but Paris breaks down in tears.

Paris: *I haven't told you this but a few weeks ago Riley assaulted someone and they were badly hurt. They ended up in A&E. The hospital called the police and eventually he was arrested. But I lied and told them he was home with me all night. They've studied CCTV footage and he was identified as the person who did it. The police have now arrested me for perverting the course of justice. I feel all those years of letting him get away with things has given him the impression that he can do what he likes. I am ashamed to admit I still tried to rescue him by lying.*

Martin: *You can't blame yourself. He is sixteen and he knows the difference between right and wrong.*

Paris: *Yes, I know he does, but I haven't helped and now I could go to prison as well.*

Islay: *Paris, thank you for sharing that and I can appreciate you are feeling in a dark hole. Would you like us as a group to look at what choices you have?*

Paris smiles through her tears and says she would.

Angie: *Oh, Paris, I do feel for you. How about being honest with the police and saying sorry? That way you will feel better and you won't be rescuing Riley. You could then tell Riley about how you've got it wrong and say sorry to him?*

Paris: *It's like I try to make things better for Riley but I just end up making it worse.*

Islay: *What do you think might be the danger if you put all your energy into trying to make things better for Riley?*

Paris: *He never learns to take responsibility.*

Angie: *Opposites don't work, so I'm guessing it's about the balance again. Making sure they feel loved by taking notice of them but not overdoing it so they know there are consequences to behaviour. But it's also about giving them choices so they can choose to do what's right.*

Kim: *The more you are being honest with yourself about what is really going on and what is motivating you then the more you are giving yourself choices. You have done such a lot of work tonight and I can imagine you are all feeling exhausted. Can I suggest that you are kind to yourself this week and don't beat yourselves up. Let's finish a little differently today, by giving the person next to you a compliment.*

The parents look a bit worried about what they are being asked to do but Kim encourages them by starting the circle off.

Kim: *Paris, you are incredibly brave, thank you for your honesty.*

Paris: *Thank you, Kim; Margaret, you pick things up really easily.*

Margaret: *Ah, thank you, Paris. Angie, you are very supportive and wise.*

Angie: *Thank you. Darren, I'm really pleased you're still coming to the group each week.*

Darren: *Thanks, Angie.*

Darren looks at Anne, and is clearly struggling to give a compliment.

Paris: *Come on, Darren, you must be able to give Anne a compliment, she is your wife.*

Darren (sarcastically): *I was just trying to pick which one to give you. Anne, you always look nice.*

Anne: *Thanks Martin, you do a brilliant job bringing up your children on your own.*

Martin: *That's kind of you to say Anne. Islay thank you for all you are doing for us.*

Islay: *Thank you everyone, this has been an excellent session where you have been honest with yourselves and supported one another. Take your questionnaires home with you and set yourself a target of moving some of the lower scores up. Next session we are going to be looking at communication. This week keep up the good work of watching your own behaviour. Listen to the words you are saying, notice the tone of your voice and the way you are speaking and have a really good week.*

Martin's head was full of what had happened in the session and hurtful memories of the past. So much had changed since Sue had left. It had been such a shock when she walked out; people had said to him 'I don't know how you do it'. Well, neither did he. What else could he do but get on with it? He had thought that there was no point in looking back at the past, but maybe he was wrong. What concerned him was that he had just started to come out of depression and raking over the past might suck him back into it. He realised that he had blanked out what Sue had put them through and this had helped him cope. There was one thing he knew for sure and that was he would make it up to the children and be the best dad he could be.

As Anne put her coffee mug on to the tray and left the room she felt a bit strange. She couldn't quite put her finger on it; it was all a bit confusing. It was probably linked to her feelings for Darren. At first she had been pleased that he had agreed to come to the group with her but now it was clear that he wasn't taking it seriously. How hurtful that he couldn't even think of a compliment for her, she had been so embarrassed. After everything that they had been through, surely he could have thought of something nice to say; everyone else had managed it. At least she had started to do things differently with the children and that meant that there was hope for the future.

 **Writing a journal can help you to recognise the positive things in your life.**

 # FOR REFLECTION

1. What did you identify you are doing well in the questionnaire?

2. Where do you spend most of your energy:
   Warm?
   Firm?
   Fair?

3. Think of an example where you have operated from these states:
   Parent
   Adult
   Child

4. What have you learned in this chapter that will help you to behave differently when your child is being violent?

# 7

# BRIEF UTTERANCE

 **Listen out for feelings.** Try to put yourself in your child's shoes and think about how they may be feeling. Ask your child 'What is it like for you?'

Islay and Kim were interested to see how the parents had coped with all the information they had been given last week. In the weekly phone call there were reports that the children seemed puzzled by their parents' behaviour. They were confused as their parents were dealing with things differently. The older children noticed that their parents were changing and at times they had become even more challenging.

The group returns for the weekly session and after making themselves a hot drink they sit down to hear what has happened in the week.

Kim: *Would anyone like to tell us how their week has been and how they have got on?*

Paris: *I felt really embarrassed about telling you what I did last week, but Kim when you said I was incredibly brave that made me feel better. It has been a tough week for me and to be honest I have struggled. But Angie phoned me and reminded me about the knitting group. I didn't want to go as I was feeling so bad about* myself. I didn't think anyone would want me near them, but Angie insisted I went along and she picked me up.

Paris smiles at Angie.

Paris: *It was really lovely and the others in the group liked some of my ideas.*

Angie: *Paris, they didn't just like your ideas, they loved them. You are so creative. We all want you to come back because it was great swapping ideas with you.*

Paris: *Thank you, Angie. It was funny because I came home and started humming round the house. Riley came in with a sour look on his face and normally I'd have been walking on eggshells trying not to upset him. I just kept doing what I was doing. I gave him some food and after he'd eaten he was about to rush out again but I said I'd like to tell him something. I think he could tell I was serious as my voice was shaking. I felt so nervous, but I knew I needed to talk to him.*

Angie nods her head in agreement and Paris smiles.

Paris: *I said I was sorry and that I'd realised that I'd got a lot wrong with him in the past. He looked a bit puzzled so I said that I'd been wrong in giving him an alibi and that I had been to the police station to put things right. I told him that I'd written a confession saying that he hadn't been at home and that I had lied. I said he needed to take responsibility for himself and that I would support him but not rescue him anymore. I finished by saying that he needed to think about his future and where he wants to be in five years time. He shrugged his shoulders and said that it was too late now to think about that as he was going to prison.*

Angie: *Is that likely to happen?*

Paris: *I don't know. It was a serious assault and he could go to prison. I told Riley that if that happened he would still have a choice. I said that it was up to him to decide whether he wants to take that path in life or whether he could see that he needs to do something different.*

Martin: *That sounds amazing. How did he take it?*

Paris: *He didn't really say anything. I did think about writing it down and giving it to him in a letter but then I decided it was better to talk to him. I have the knitting group to thank for that; it has given me confidence. He's been a lot quieter since then and I haven't had any problems with him. I think he is worried and I've noticed that I keep getting sucked in. I want to make him feel better by saying 'Don't worry, it'll be all right', but I keep hearing Islay's voice saying 'What will you teach him?' and I manage to stop myself just in time. I've realised that he needs to experience this horrible feeling.*

Martin: *That sounds a bit tough.*

Paris: *I know it does, and I'm not sure how to explain it. But I have this horrid feeling all the time in the pit of my stomach and he does whatever he wants to do. I've realised that for him to change he needs to experience the same worry as I have been. It's not me making him feel it; this is something he's brought on himself.*

Martin: *I think I get it. Is it a bit like taking their PE kit to school so they don't experience the detention?*

Kim: *Yes it is just like that. It's much easier for them to experience this over small things like the PE kit and much harder when there is more at stake. Paris you have done a fantastic job with Riley, you were very clear and you have given him choices. You won't be able to stop worrying about him; you love him and want what's best for him. What you have started to do though is to change your* behaviour and let him take on some of that worry. It's not enough for you to want what's best for Riley; he needs to want what is best for him as well.

Islay: *Martin, how did you get on with the spare forms?*

Martin: *It was interesting. I've realised I am a lot softer on Lucy and Jessie than the boys. The other day I heard Jessie start to cry and she shouted out, 'John's hit me'. She must have thought I was in the kitchen but I had just come into the room and she hadn't realised. I was really shocked as John was on the other side of the room and she was sat on the sofa. I just looked at her and her face was a picture. I told her to go to her room and think about what she needed to say to John for blaming him for something he hadn't done. John looked relieved. It's got me thinking about the times I have come down really hard on John, giving him a lecture about how you don't hit women and how you must respect them. He would tell me he hadn't hit Jessie but I never believed him. I realised I needed to talk to him so we went out for a walk and I said sorry. John seemed really happy and we went on to talk about how tricky younger sisters can be.*

Paris: *Wow, Martin you are such a lovely dad, they are so lucky to have you. I wish Riley's dad had been half as understanding as you.*

Islay: *Not being believed is really hard and leaves you with the feeling of isolation. It's difficult as an adult to have people not understand your motives and to believe wrong things about you, but it is exceptionally hard for children. We can't believe everything our children say and we do have to check out the evidence. What you have talked about is a very common problem between siblings and it can be very difficult to know which child to believe.*

Anne: *I realise I have been quite distant to Mikki. I've been around for her but it was what you said last week Angie that made me* think. It was about going through the motions of parenting Harry. I'm wondering if that is what I have been doing with Mikki. I had three children already when I got pregnant with Mikki so I guess it was a distraction for me. I didn't know what I was going to do with my life. I'd never worked and when my husband died it was really hard. I think I had been used to being looked after and suddenly I was on my own. Darren came into my life at just the right time.

Darren looks a bit puzzled.

Darren: *It doesn't feel like that now.*

Anne looks at Darren and continues:

Anne: *I know and I recognise that this is a difficult time for us right now. I'm not the same person as I was then and I think I have left you to be the main carer for Mikki. I didn't have any more energy left to give her. I realise that she probably sensed it and maybe that's one of the reasons she can be so difficult.*

Darren: *I always felt you've been a bit distant to her and would go and sort Sophie out at a drop of a hat. Mikki was just left to sort herself out.*

Martin: *I have the feeling that you two aren't very happy and it's hard to understand what is next for you both. After my wife Sue walked out I found it really hard to cope. Kyle was only a baby and I didn't know what to do. One of Sue's friends kept coming round and she was really good at getting the kids sorted. I sort of left her to it. Eventually she came round and you know how it is, we had a bit to drink, the kids were asleep and we ended up in bed together. It lasted for over a year. In that time the kids really started to play up, especially John. He became so disruptive at school and he would swear at the teachers. If he didn't want to do something he wouldn't do it and he was always getting excluded. I'd get a phone call from* the school almost every day. In some ways it was easier when he refused to go to school. At least I could leave him in bed and get on with looking after the others. It's been a bit of a nightmare.

Paris: *That's like Riley. I used to dread the phone going during the day. Didn't the school fine you?*

Martin: *I kept going to the school and telling them I didn't know what to do. I think they felt sorry for me and they were really supportive. They got John a youth worker and they'd go out together. I suppose it gave me a bit of peace for a few hours, but John wasn't that interested. I'm not sure it helped. He'd come home and his behaviour was just as bad as ever.*

Paris: *That's typical, I'm sure they felt sorry for you because you're a single dad. Riley's school is so judgmental of me. They probably thought you're a single dad who's doing his best and needs support. The school did nothing for Riley and I've had to fight for everything. They took me to court and were going to fine me for not getting Riley to school. I was lucky; the judge was really kind and told the school they needed to get me some support.*

Kim: *What support did you get?*

Paris: *Well ... they referred me to this group.*

The group laughs.

Martin: *Yes, they referred me to the group as well. John has been diagnosed with ADHD and he is under the Child and Adolescent Mental Health Services.*

Angie: *Has he got a mental health problem then?*

Martin: *Well I think he has as he can switch at a drop of a hat.*

*It's like he's two different people. One minute he can be lovely and the next minute he's a raving lunatic. Most of the doors have holes in them.*

Angie: *That sounds like my brother. I didn't think ADHD was a mental illness though. He had ADHD and he was monitored through the GP. He was given tablets and it did seem to calm him down a bit. It didn't stop him being horrid at times, especially to me.*

Islay: *It's very hard to know what is causing challenging behaviour. Children with ADHD are very impulsive and have little or no fear of danger. However ADHD does not mean a disrespectful or rude child. Some parents think that if their child has a diagnosis of ADHD then that explains their behaviour. Even if your child has a diagnosis their behaviour still has to be managed. What I think we have heard today is that by doing something different yourself you start to get a different outcome.*

Martin: *That's true. I asked John if he wanted to go fishing. I have a friend who is always going fishing so I asked him if we could join him one day. It was so good, I'd never done it before and we both loved it. I spoke to the youth worker about it and there's a charity that takes parents and children fishing so we've joined up and we've arranged it with the school to go for a couple of hours when Kyle is at nursery.*

Kim: *Martin, can I ask what John's behaviour has been like since then?*

Martin: *In a funny sort of way it has been much better. I've realised that when his sisters have a go at him and he is about to have a go back at them I can distract him by talking about fishing. It helps to keep him calm, although sometimes it doesn't work because he is easy prey for them. The one thing I have noticed is that Jessie has started to play up. It's almost like they have switched roles.*

Islay: *It is really interesting when that happens and it is something that is quite common in families. This links back to the messages that we have received and the labels that we were given by our parents. These labels are a description of our behaviour, so you may describe your child as:*

- *The Difficult one*
- *The Helpful one*
- *The Princess*
- *The Comic*
- *The Inquisitive one.*

*The list could go on. The labels describe how we get our needs met. What you have described is what happens when one child takes on the label of another sibling. If the way your child gets attention is by being helpful and your other child's way of getting attention is being difficult, then if the difficult one starts to be helpful, that will challenge the helpful one and they may become difficult. It is common for children in the family to swap labels; when it seems like you have got one child's difficult behaviour sorted another child's behaviour becomes difficult. This can be very challenging to parents because it feels like things are getting worse.*

Martin: *That's exactly what is happening.*

 **I'm sorry you feel that way.** When your child says unkind and hurtful things to you, instead of justifying your behaviour, simply say 'I am sorry you feel that way'. When you begin to challenge your child's words in a kind way they begin to think about what they are saying.

Kim: *I think this session on communication will really help you to get some positive messages across to John. To understand what our children are hearing us say we are going to look at the different ways we communicate with them. Can anyone tell me one way that we communicate with each other?*

Paris: *Well I talk. Not that Riley bothers to listen.*

Islay: *What do you think Riley does listen to?*

Paris: *My body language.*

Kim: *We think what we say is important, and it is to us, but that isn't what people listen to.*

Kim draws the first triangle on the flip chart.

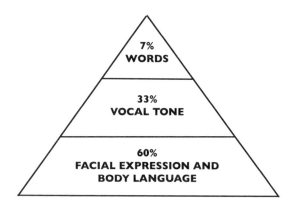

Kim: *If you see someone crying, for example, what do you instantly think?*

Anne: *They're upset, hurt or sad about something.*

Paris: *If I cry it usually means I'm angry.*

Islay: *Yes, they are all possible, which could be confusing. Especially if you saw Paris crying and went to comfort her because you thought she was sad about something and she was angry.*

Paris (laughing): *Yes, I might end up having a right go at you.*

Kim: *If you see someone who is smiling what do you think may be going on for them?*

Anne: *That they're happy.*

Martin: *I was thinking that they could be embarrassed. When I was younger I was caught shoplifting and I had to go to the police station. I was arrested and the Inspector gave me a right telling off. He was really fierce and it was then I realised what a prat I'd been. I was really embarrassed and for some reason I found myself smiling. The Inspector became angry when I smiled as he thought I was messing around and I nearly went to court. It was only because I nearly broke down that he let me off. It was awful at the time but it shows how I was giving out the wrong message. I was terrified but I ended up smiling.*

Islay: *Not a very nice experience for you, but actually very common for people to experience. Sometimes you can find yourself smiling when you're telling someone bad news.*

Anne: *Gosh, I hadn't realised that. When Roy died I had to tell people and I could feel myself smiling. I'm sure people thought I was heartless but I felt terrible.*

Kim: *It can be very confusing. This links in to the Window to Self-Knowledge. When we understand more about how we communicate and the messages we are giving out it will help us to understand our Boxes 3 and 4.*

Angie: *So are you saying that sometimes our words don't match up with our body language?*

Islay: *Yes that's exactly what we are saying. If you look at the diagram it's not just what we say but how we say it that people will tune into. Can you give me an example of someone saying something but meaning the opposite?*

Anne: *I can – last week when Darren was trying to pay me a compliment.*

Darren looks upset.

Paris: *Yes, that did sound a bit insincere*

Kim: *How can you tell if someone is being insincere?*

Margaret: *I think it's when they're being sarcastic. I often hear sarcasm when people talk to me.*

Angie: *Is it possible that you sometimes think people are being sarcastic and they're not?*

Margaret: *I don't think so, why?*

Angie: *Well, sometimes we've tried to pay you a compliment and you brush it off. I wonder if you think we don't mean it, that we're just saying it and it's not true.*

Margaret: *Oh. I am always suspicious when someone gives me a compliment. I question why they would do that and what they are after.*

Angie: *Do you think that links back to when you were a child and you were paid compliments but that meant awful things for you?*

Margaret: *I suppose so; I hadn't really thought about it.*

Paris: *People say I sound angry and my friend says I speak harshly to Riley.*

Paris is quite thoughtful.

Margaret: *That's made me think more about what I hear when people speak to me. When the school talks to me about Damien I come away feeling like they are judging me.*

Anne: *Oh, Margaret, that must be really difficult for you. You have shared such a lot and have been so brave. It's such a shame if you don't believe it when people are either trying to help you or pay you a compliment.*

Margaret smiles and is clearly thinking about what has been said.

Kim: *We've discussed body language, words and how we say them. Now we are going to use another triangle to look at the different levels of communication we use.*

Islay draws a triangle on the flipchart and divides it into 5 sections.

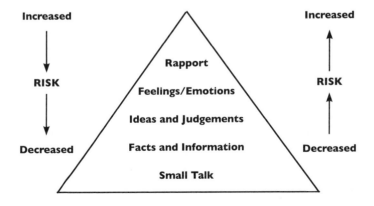

*Islay: What we talk about is often determined by who we are talking to and whether we trust them or not. Can anyone give an example of when you might use small talk?*

Anne: *Today there were lots of people waiting for the bus and we were talking about it being late and how the weather has changed.*

Islay: *Thank you, Anne. If you move up to the next level, this is where we give facts and information.*

Martin: *Is that like me telling the children where I've put their clothes?*

Kim: *Yes, that's it. Pub quizzes are also a good example of people who would share facts and information.*

Islay: *The next level of communication is where we start to share our ideas and judgments about things or people.*

Paris: *I think that's where I get into trouble. I'm always ready to say exactly what I think, especially at the school. I have the reputation of going there and yelling at the teachers.*

Margaret: *I'm always too scared to share my ideas. I think people will think I'm stupid.*

Kim refers to the arrows either side of the triangle, which are labeled trust and risk.

Kim: *The diagram shows how our levels of trust and risk increase as we move up through the levels of communication. It links to what you have just said Margaret, it can be difficult to trust people enough to open up to them and share our ideas. The risks are greater at this level because by sharing yourself you leave yourself open and vulnerable to others.*

Islay: *That brings us to the next level of feelings and emotions. Does anyone know the difference?*

Martin: *I've suffered from depression for a long time and I had some counselling a year ago. My counsellor explained that emotions are short-lived and reactive whereas feelings are more underlying and longer lasting. He said that the feeling I was experiencing was depression but I would have other emotions which were a reaction to circumstances. It was a bit complicated but I sort of got it. I have suffered from depression for many years, but I was doing okay and then my wife left and I couldn't cope and I felt sad. The sadness was hard to manage so instead of being able to recognise what I was doing well, it turned into depression.*

Paris: *I've never thought of it like that. So is it possible that I love Riley so much, my feeling is love, but when he does something I get really angry with him. Like when he was arrested. Because I love him it made me frightened for him, which then prompted me to rescue him by lying.*

Islay: *Yes those are both really good descriptions. Love is the feeling and your reaction of anger is based on fear.*

Darren: *So what? It doesn't make any difference to the outcome whether it is a feeling or emotion.*

Islay: *Well, it may or it may not. That is dependent on each person. However, if we want to become more aware of Boxes 3 and 4 in the Window to Self-Knowledge, it is good to work out what our motivation is and how that can then dictate our behaviour.*

Paris: *Well it's beginning to make perfect sense to me. The way I have shown that I love Riley is usually out of fear as I am frightened of what might happen to him. When I am afraid I get cross and angry. He probably hears the anger rather than the love I feel for him.*

Kim: *Well done Paris. So then finally we come to Rapport. Has anyone any idea what that means? Being in rapport with someone?*

Angie: *Philip says it's when I finish his sentence for him. I hope he's joking but for me it's about empathy, understanding someone and not judging them.*

Islay: *It's really important to work out where you are on the triangle when you are communicating with your children. What level do you think parents generally communicate from?*

Angie: *Telling children what to do and what they're doing wrong.*

Islay: *Yes, without realising it we tend to get stuck at the facts and information level with ideas and judgments thrown in for good measure. This kind of communication comes across as negative.*

Paris: *Oh dear, that sounds like me. I say to Riley. 'You have to get up at seven o'clock and then get the bus and if you don't you won't learn anything, people will think you are stupid and you'll never get a decent job.'*

Margaret: *But you say that to him because you love him and you are worried about what he will do with the rest of his life?*

Paris smiles at Margaret and nods her head. She is grateful that someone else understands her and is not judging her.

Kim: *Parents often get stuck on the lower levels. What level do you think our children communicate from?*

Anne: *Mikki gets really angry with me so that would be on the emotion level.*

The other parents nod and agree that their children are often angry and emotional.

Kim: *Yes, children don't often have the words to express their feelings but they will show you how they feel in other ways,*

Angie: *Like slamming doors, throwing things? That is how Harry reacts to me when I give him advice. This is making sense to me and I think I need to do something differently.*

Kim: *We know that children can quite easily communicate from an emotional level and that parents generally offer their children advice and opinions. To improve communication our children need us to take a risk and share our feelings with them.*

Margaret: *That is really scary.*

Islay: *Yes it is, but what will happen if you don't?*

Martin: *They could end up rebelling against us.*

Islay: *However scary we may find it we need to communicate honestly with our children. We need to do this in a way that tells them how to change their behaviour, without them feeling like they are useless. The other important factor is to think about how our children may be feeling.*

Angie: *I use the 'sounds like you're feeling…' approach. It really works with Harry as he soon tells me if I've got the feeling wrong. It encourages him to talk, as I'm not judging him, I'm just making a statement.*

Margaret: *I find it hard to remember to do all this when I'm getting angry.*

Kim: *Changing our behaviour feels awkward at first and we really have to think about it. The great thing is it gets more comfortable with time and becomes automatic the more you practice.*

**An 'I statement' is a calm, direct way of communicating.** Work out what you want to say, write it down if it helps and then deliver it with belief in yourself. Practice this whenever you can:

I feel ............................... (name your feeling)
When you ..................... (name the behaviour)
Because it is important to/that ........................
(the reason for a change in behaviour )
I would like you to................................(the preferred behaviour)

Islay: *Telling your children how you feel can be very effective. Can anyone give an example?*

Margaret: *I usually say to Damien, 'You never get up on time for school; I am fed up of telling you'. I guess he doesn't want to hear that any more. I'm wondering whether I could say, 'Damien, I feel worried when you don't get up for school, because it is important to get an education. I would like you to get up on time tomorrow.' What do you think?*

Angie: *For someone who doesn't like to share her ideas I think you have done brilliantly. That sounds amazing.*

Margaret has a big smile on her face.

Anne: *I'm really impressed, Margaret.*

Kim: *One thing to remember is that our children want to please* us. They don't want our displeasure. Often all we tell them is what they are doing wrong so it's really helpful to them when we can tell them what we want them to do and what they are doing right. It's about encouraging them, not blaming them.

Islay: *In this session we have looked at different ways that we communicate. What do you think you can do differently this week?*

Paris: *I'm going to show Riley the communication triangle. I'm going to ask him to help me work out where we both are on the triangle.*

Margaret: *I'm going to change what I say to Damien about school.*

Anne: *I want to concentrate on matching my body language to my words, especially with Sophie. I know I have been feeling guilty so I just do anything she wants me to. I realise that she takes advantage of me. I'm going to try and be honest about my feelings and really work out when I am reacting emotionally.*

Darren: *You don't seem to have any problem matching your body language to your words with me. I don't know about all this, I just feel churned up and if I'm honest a bit fed up. It has been good to talk to Martin though.*

Martin: *We blokes understand each other. Perhaps we're in rapport.*

The group chuckle, but Martin has a point. Men and women will often communicate in a different way and have different expectations.

Martin: *Seriously though. This has got me thinking. Some of the stuff I already knew but had forgotten. I know how easy it is for me to slip back into depression so it's been really helpful talking about it. It was good to go over the difference between feelings and emotions again. As the kids are getting bigger the house seems to be getting smaller. I find if I keep thinking about it then it smothers me, whereas if I can focus on other things then it doesn't overwhelm me. I'm going to continue finding positive things to say to the children. I want us to be in rapport. Who knows I might end up knowing what they are thinking.*

That makes everyone laugh.

Angie: *Again, it has been really interesting. I have learnt so much since coming here. I had no idea how complicated communication is, it almost makes me scared to open my mouth. I think Harry must be confused by my behaviour. I'm going to really think about the levels of communication, not only with him but also with my mum who can be very judgmental towards me.*

Darren watched the other parents as they left the room and wondered what had just happened. He had come to the group to support Anne and now it seemed like he had become the problem. What Anne had said in front of everyone had shocked and hurt him. He was still trying to make sense of it. It was good when Anne told everyone that he had come into her life at the right time, it was the 'sort yourself out' bit that had hit him hard. That's when it had become really awkward for him, he had started to feel out of control and that was not a good feeling. It was lucky that Martin was there to break the silence and take the pressure off of him.

Margaret was feeling hopeful as she took her coat from the back of the chair and slipped it on. After the last few sessions, which had left her reeling, this one had been okay. At home things were more comfortable too. Damien was more settled and she had stopped walking on eggshells to avoid conflict. The 'Donkey' word had helped to release some tension between them and there had been fewer violent episodes. As Margaret left the room she smiled at how much she was enjoying the group; it was so interesting to hear everyone's stories and to see the changes they were making. Margaret wondered what she would do when the group sessions came to an end.

 **Think about how you behave towards a really good friend that you like and give yourself the same attention.**

 ## FOR REFLECTION

1. What messages did you receive as a child?

2. Were they positive or negative or a mixture of both?

3. What messages are you giving to your child?

4. What have you learned in this chapter that will help you to behave differently when your child is being violent?

# 8

# THE DIRECTOR'S CUT

 **Ask questions.** Show that you are interested in your child's life by asking questions and listening to what they have to say. Learn about their goals, dreams and wishes.

When Islay and Kim contacted the parents for the weekly phone call the parents were much more honest with them. Darren and Anne were struggling. Anne told Kim that she had moved into the spare room and that the week had been a struggle as Darren had been angry most of the time. She had asked him to go to couple counselling with her but so far he had refused. It seemed as if he wasn't prepared to do anything to save their marriage. Anne knew that she couldn't go back to behaving in the same way as she had before, especially for Mikki's sake. Anne was left wondering what this meant for her and Darren. Darren was not available for the weekly phone call.

*

Everyone arrives at the group and they start to chat to each other. Some of the parents have become friends on Facebook and the topic of conversation is Paris's latest night out. Kim starts the session by asking them how their week has been. There is general laughter as they are still talking about Paris's night out.

Paris: *Yes, well I went out. I had a really great night and met this guy. He was gorgeous and so considerate. He wouldn't let me leave on my own and insisted when we left the club that he walked on the side of the cars. I have never been treated like that. It was amazing. He's been texting me since then saying that he wants to meet up again.*

Kim: *How lovely for you. So how are things with Riley?*

Paris: *Well he was a bit sour-faced in the morning. I don't know what his problem is. You'd think he'd be pleased I'd met someone. At least it will take the focus off of him; it might stop me nagging him.*

Kim: *So if you think about last week, the way we communicate and what message our children might be getting from our behaviour, how might Riley be feeling?*

Paris: *I don't know. He never seems happy for me.*

Angie: *Could it be that he is not thinking about you in this, so it's not personal. What I mean is that he's not upset that you've met someone, he's fearful of what that might mean for him. Your attention is on someone else?*

Martin: *I remember when I was younger and dad left. Mum used to have different boyfriends. It was really awkward. I knew that mum needed company but some of the men were pretty awful. They would start off caring for her but fairly soon they would start putting demands on her. Mum would end up in tears and it was always me that had to comfort her. I used to dread her saying that she'd met someone. I can still remember the last time. I got so angry when she came back and told me that she'd met another bloke. I smashed up the sitting room. Then I stormed out. I was older by that time so I started sleeping on friends' sofas. Eventually they got fed up with me and I had to go and get some help. It was a really awful time in my* life. I get on much better now with my mum and she's really helpful with my children but at the time sparks would really fly.

Paris: So didn't you want your mum to find someone? It must have been hard for her after you left. I mean I know children do leave but what am I supposed to do?

Martin: It wasn't about that. It was about the fact that she always picked the wrong men and then they'd leave her. A couple of them were pretty violent towards her and I got scared each time. I always felt she was vulnerable and I needed to look after her. I felt awful walking away but I knew it wasn't doing me any good staying, as I was getting so angry.

Angie: Have you talked to your mum about it since?

Martin: Yes. She was trying to tell me to go and find someone to help me with the kids. I couldn't believe it and before I knew it I'd snapped back at her 'You mean like you did when I was growing up?' In fairness she did apologise which I found a bit difficult. I know that the past is gone and telling her how awful it was wouldn't change anything, so for her to say sorry was enough for me. We've actually got on much better since then. It seems like she's changed from back then, in a funny sort of way she's happy with her life and doesn't want to go out and try and find a man.

Paris: Oh. I need to think about this. Thanks Martin, it's helpful hearing about it from your point of view.

Martin: It's worth thinking about. It took me ages to get a better relationship with my mum. It's okay now and she is a fantastic grandmother. Sometimes it hurts when I see her cuddling my children; I think why couldn't you have done that to me? It was like she wanted her cuddles from a man and it left me thinking I was a nuisance.

Angie: *That's really sad, Martin and I hadn't thought that children would see things so differently. It's really good that you've got a better relationship now with your mum. Do you think that when we become parents we want the opposite of what we had for our kids?*

Martin: *Yes, it's only now that I realise it though. It was last week that it came home to me. I hadn't realised how much I reacted from my past. I catch myself now when I'm feeling cross and I'm learning to stop and ask myself why. In fact I was starting to get annoyed with the kids last night because when they came home, they wouldn't put anything away and they were really annoying and winding each other up. So I called them together, sat them down and said that I could feel myself getting cross and I wanted their help to work out why, so maybe we could have a brainstorming session to find out all the possible reasons. They thought I was mad; I got a piece of paper and went round everyone asking them all to come up with a reason. It ended up being quite funny. I was really surprised at how switched on they were and they all agreed it was because they weren't doing what I had asked. I asked them why and they said it was probably because it had been raining and they hadn't been allowed out in the playground. I told them I was very impressed that they had worked that out but as it wasn't my fault that it was raining they needed to find another way of dealing with all the energy. I asked them if they could come up with a solution. They decided that they could all do some star jumps for 2 minutes. They immediately got up and loved it. We had such a good evening after that.*

Kim: *Well done. That was a great way of developing rapport. You didn't keep giving them orders; you listened to your emotions, you shared them appropriately and then you heard everyone's point of view. That's brilliant and I'm not surprised that you had a good evening after that.*

Margaret: *I've kept saying to Damien about going to school. He just looks at me and says 'Yeah, whatever'. It's been quite hard to keep it up. The first morning he just ignored what I said and he got up late.*

*He eventually went to school but it took quite a lot of nagging from me. The school said that if Damien refuses to get up in the morning, I should ring them and say in a loud voice that he's refusing to get up. That way he'll know that I'm not going to make excuses for him. The next morning instead of nagging him I just told him that if he didn't get up in 5 minutes I would ring the school and tell them he was refusing to get up. Of course he didn't think that I would do it. I was really nervous but I phoned the school and told them. They were lovely and said thank you for letting them know. Damien was furious and started yelling at me. It was very tempting to go back to the nagging but I realised that I would have then slipped back on that triangle. I just said I'm sorry you don't like what I have done but you do have a choice. He was really grumpy and refused to go to school. I was really upset but I still rung the school. I wasn't sure if I was doing the right thing, at least he was going in before and now he wasn't going in at all. The school were great and said not to worry and they knew what I was trying to do and would support me. The next morning I went in and woke him up. He started to have a moan so I said that if he wasn't out of bed in 5 minutes I would ring the school again. I told him I'd made some toast for him and then I left the room. He did get up eventually, he came downstairs ate his toast and I just managed to get him to school as the bell rang. After I dropped him off I spoke to the teacher and they were delighted and kept saying how well I was doing. I felt really good. He's been better since then and now whenever I say how important education is, instead of saying 'Yeah, whatever' he says 'I know'. He seems to be enjoying school because he came home with a card, which said how well he'd done with his reading. I felt really proud of him and I told him too.*

*Paris: Wow, Margaret. You are amazing. And I think that's the longest you've spoken. I need to copy what you have done.*

*Margaret: Well the school have asked me if I would talk to another parent who is really struggling to get their child to school. I've told her that she needs to come and do this course.*

Margaret looks much happier and is clearly growing in confidence. She has come such a long way since she started the course. For the first time in her life she is beginning to feel that she has something to say and she no longer feels alone.

Kim: *The session this week is about behaviour. It links back to what needs our children are getting met by behaving in a certain way. There are a few exercises that we are going to do to find out what is going on and what we can do differently. We are going to begin by looking at what may be underneath your child's behaviour.*

Darren(sarcastically): *Finally. We're looking at our child's behaviour rather than ours.*

Islay gives the parents a piece of flip chart paper with an iceberg drawn on it. The top of the iceberg has 'SEEN' written above it and the iceberg that is under the water has 'UNSEEN' written across it. Following instructions the parents write the behaviours that their children use in the top section of the iceberg (what is seen). They identify all of the negative behaviours and there is a lot of violence in all forms.

Angie: *Do we write positive behaviour or just negative?*

Islay: *Yes, that is a good point Angie. Write all of the behaviour that you see, so that will be both negative and positive.*

After a while Kim asks the parents to write on the UNSEEN section of the paper any reasons why children may behave in that way. This would include any external factors, and internal factors such as the values, beliefs and messages that they had discussed in earlier sessions. The parents begin to scratch their heads and there are some in-depth conversations going on. Eventually they start to write.

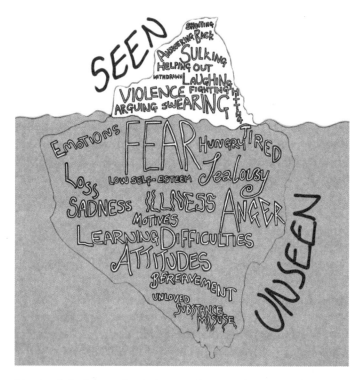

Martin: *I hadn't realised that tiredness or hunger could trigger their behaviour. I get really grumpy if I'm hungry, so it's no surprise that they might be like that as well.*

Paris: *I hadn't thought about bereavement having an impact. I had thought how the breakdown of relationships would, but not someone dying. When my Gran died I was heartbroken, but Riley didn't really know her so I didn't think it would've had much of an impact on him.*

Kim: *It might have got muddled in his head because you were so upset and you may have found it hard to cope. Our children react to our feelings so if we're okay then they tend to feel okay, but if we're struggling it can affect them.*

Angie: *You said earlier that behaviour is about getting your needs met, so we could be asking what need are they getting met by behaving in this way.*

Islay: *Yes, can you give us an example of that?*

Angie: *I think back to when Philip and I were arguing a lot and how Harry was at that time. I think he worked out that if he played up then he would get our attention. If he sat quietly we sort of forgot about him. It sounds awful but we were so wrapped up in our problems that it was easier for us if he sat watching TV or playing a game on his Xbox. He'd refuse to come and eat when I needed him to or he would refuse to go to bed and I'd get impatient. At one point I thought there must be something wrong with him. I asked the school if he could be tested for dyslexia, dyspraxia, ADD, ADHD, anything that would explain his behaviour. They just said that they didn't have a problem with him at school and it wasn't necessary to get him tested. I even took him to my GP to try and get him referred. He wasn't particularly helpful. I was really stuck with this badly behaved child and no one seemed to care. It was a really awful time.*

Margaret: *How is it now?*

Angie: *Well things are definitely better. We still have our moments and I'm beginning to understand that a lot of what Harry was going through was his way of coping. As adults we behave differently when we are upset so why wouldn't our children? I just hadn't realised that the way Philip and I were behaving towards each other would have such an impact on Harry.*

Paris: *Oh dear, I think I'm beginning to see why Riley might have got so upset with me going out. It is such a balance between enjoying yourself but not at the expense of your children. I wonder if I'll ever be able to go out and not worry what Riley will think.*

Kim: *We have to be a bit careful here as this isn't about not doing things for the fear of what our children will make of it. They won't like it when we put in rules and boundaries and that's okay as long as the rules and boundaries are reasonable. It's when they're not reasonable that they will feel life is unfair.*

Paris: *That sounds like me. I try to put in a consequence and then I never stick to it. Riley kicks off in such a big way. He can get really threatening and as I've said before he'll get right in my face. In the end I'm so scared that I give in but I'm also really angry that he's made me feel like that. He knows I haven't got much money but he expects me to give him a fiver every day for his lunch. He says he won't go to school if I don't give it to him, so in the end I give it to him.*

Islay: *That sounds as if he is blackmailing you. He is getting a payoff from behaving in that way. Do you know what need he's getting met?*

Angie: *Harry got my attention; but it was negative attention as I was telling him off. I'm guessing that was his need for attention being met.*

Paris: *Riley is trying to take control.*

Angie: *It comes back to balance again. You both need to feel in control. I know as Harry grows I have to find a way of giving him some control. It is really hard. When they are younger you have to make their decisions for them. I remember once when Harry was 3 he went to run out into the road. I was so worried that I screamed at him. When I got hold of him I smacked him. Then I felt awful as I always said I'd never do that so I gave him a hug. Thinking about it now, how confusing was that.*

Paris: *Crikey, I've done that too.*

Islay: *It is hard and they are very natural reactions. Your fear prompts your actions. But if we give such mixed messages, our children have to try and make sense of it. They will soon learn that they can manipulate us.*

Martin: *So if we say no to our children and then we give in to them our children are learning that our no doesn't mean no. If they nag us enough it might mean yes.*

Paris (defensively): *I don't always give in.*

Kim: *Children are opportunists and they will have a go at trying to persuade you. They seem to instinctively know when no means no and when no might mean 'possibly' or even 'yes'.*

Martin: *I think I've been guilty of that. The girls are more likely to get a yes from me.*

Darren: *So is Mikki, she just has a way about her that is very persuasive. I have this thought in my head which says 'no' but then I find myself saying 'okay'. It's usually before tea is ready and she says that she wants a packet of crisps. I think 'no' at first then I find myself saying 'Well, okay as long as you promise to eat your tea'. She'll say she will eat her tea and then she doesn't and we end up having an argument.*

Islay: *So what might you be able to do differently?*

Darren (sarcastically): *Say no and stick to it?*

Islay: *Yes, but you could soften it by saying something like, 'I know you're hungry but tea won't be long. Would you like to help stir the pot?' This would be getting her involved in some way.*

Darren likes that idea and Kim and Islay are pleased that he's joined in. He had previously been looking very fed up and uninterested in what was going on around him.

Anne: *Sophie used to just flip; I never knew when it was coming. I always felt like I was walking on eggshells and she is still a bit like that. I don't know what she is getting from that behaviour.*

Margaret: *Damien was like that. He'd be watching TV and then all of a sudden he would start. I could never understand why.*

Angie: *It's interesting because what I think you've been saying is that behaviour doesn't come from nowhere.*

 **Children need to know where the limits are so that they feel secure.** They will always push the boundaries, they are testing you out, and this is part of normal development. Keep the boundaries consistent so that your child learns how to set their own boundaries.

Kim: *It is really hard sometimes to work out why they are kicking off. The more we are able to stop ourselves from getting sucked in and we are able to take a step back, the more we are able to see the warning signs.*

Islay: *Behaviour usually starts a bit like a play. There's a beginning, middle and an end and you probably know your own script very well. We would like you to share your experiences with each other by writing a play and acting it out.*

Some of the parents look horrified at what they are being asked to do and some are keen to demonstrate the behaviour that they have had to put with for a long time.

Islay: *Can you decide on a subject, talk about what normally happens and how it would end. Then choose who is going to play what happens.*

There is a murmur in the room as they decide on the behaviour they are going to use. It is difficult to choose, as there are so many that they can pick from.

Martin moves to the centre of the room enthusiastically while Darren follows behind reluctantly. Martin explains that he is going to play himself and Darren would be playing the part of John. The play begins:

John opens the door and slams his way in. He throws his bag on the floor.

Martin: *Pick your bag up and stop the attitude.*

John (halfway out of the other door): *Do it yourself.*

Martin (shouting): *Don't talk to me like that. Come back and pick your bag up.*

John: *SOD OFF!*

Martin: *HOW DARE YOU TALK TO ME LIKE THAT!*

Martin immediately grabs hold of John and drags him back to the bag. They are squaring up to each other and you can feel the anger in the room. The others are all a bit shocked.

Kim: *Martin, Darren, thank you. What great acting skills, that was very powerful.*

Martin and Darren start smiling at each other and go and

sit down. Kim asks the group about the scene they have just witnessed.

Kim: *What would you say was the first thing that happened in the play?*

Paris: *When John came in he was angry.*

Margaret: *That's exactly how Damien comes in.*

Kim: *What might have happened to John before he came home to make him angry?*

Angie: *His girlfriend could have just dumped him.*

Martin (laughing): *Girlfriend? He's only 12.*

Darren: *He was bullied on his way home.*

Margaret: *He'd played up at school and he knew that his teacher was going to ring his dad.*

Kim: *Yes, any of these things could have happened and maybe something else that you haven't thought about. Something has happened, you just don't know what.*

Angie: *So, the first indication that something isn't okay for them might be when they first come home?*

Kim: *Yes, and that's information for parents. Clearly it's not okay for your child to take it out on you and they will need help to manage their emotions. So knowing that, what do you think Martin could do to help John?*

Anne: *When he comes home could you say something like 'Looks as if you've had a bad day'?*

Paris: *Or maybe say nothing but offer him a drink. That way he'll know you care and then you can talk to him about putting his bag away later.*

Kim: *They are great suggestions, thank you. It's really important and essential that the boundaries are in place. What we saw in the play was that the relationship was damaged. Martin did get John to pick up the bag but it was done in anger. What does that teach John?*

Martin: *That anger gets things done.*

Paris: *It is a tricky one as anger often does get things done but I understand your point about the relationship being damaged.*

Anne: *It comes back to balance again, doesn't it? What are we teaching our child? What is the message coming across? And can we get them to do things without getting angry?*

Martin: *So, when we operate out of anger it means we insist things are done in our way and in our time.*

Kim: *Yes, ideally you would want the bag put away as soon as they come home, but as you have discovered, shouting and getting cross may get the job done but at what cost? As parents if we can see that something has upset our child we need to ask ourselves what is more important right at this minute. Is it more important for your child to know that you understand they're upset, even if you can't make it better for them, or that their bag gets put away?*

Paris: *Put like that it makes sense. I guess some things can wait.*

Islay: *Well, what if you come home and you're tired, work has been awful and you feel fed up. If someone noticed and said to you 'You look tired, go and put your feet up and I'll make you a cup of tea', how would you feel?*

Paris: *Like I'd died and gone to heaven.*

The group laugh. They are beginning to realise that their children are just like they are.

Islay: *We all have pressures upon us which cause us stress and we also have our own emotions to manage. When your child comes home and they are angry it probably has nothing to do with you. The battle comes when you assume that your child wants the same thing as you do, often they don't. It may be really important to you that your child puts their bag away but for your child putting their bag away is not a priority.*

Islay: *This play has shown us the traps that we can fall into, how we can get sucked into behaving in the same way as we have always done. If we keep doing the same thing then our children will learn a pattern of behaviour and this will keep happening until someone decides to change it. Think about what normally plays out between you and your child.*

Kim: *Most parents want their child to change before they do, but as we have discovered in this play, a child, or adult, is not likely to change if they don't need to.*

Martin: *Yes, why would our children change when we are giving them what they think they want?*

Martin: *I'm wondering if we choose our children's friends.*

There's a snort of laughter around the room.
Martin (smiling): *Just bear with me for a moment. Think about it.*

*If our children ask for things and we give them to them, then that will start their interest off and they will follow that topic. They are likely to make friends who also share that interest. I'm thinking about John. He has become really interested in fishing since I took him and he's linked in with some people at school who also enjoy fishing. He now talks about his new friends instead of his old ones and it's all fishing talk.*

Paris: *I've never really thought about it before and I guess with Riley I just left him to develop his own interests.*

Angie: *Children do need guiding though so I guess it's about finding something they are interested in and supporting them but not pushing them. Harry loves his football and I really struggle as I find football so boring. I also get cold standing watching the games. Fortunately his dad loves it and so he goes with him, it's their thing that they do together. Mind you it hasn't always been like that. He used to get cross with Harry if he missed a shot and then Harry didn't want to go anymore. It was about the same time as Phillip lost his job. It's funny, it was almost as if he felt a failure being made redundant and then somehow made Harry feel like that when he missed a shot.*

Islay: *Well done, Angie; you are beginning to see how unknowingly we pass on our emotions to our children. If we are enthusiastic about something, then the chances are they will become enthusiastic as well. It will all change once our children hit puberty. That's normal, but once they are through it they usually come back to what we have initially taught them.*

Anne: *Yes that is true. Sophie makes me feel guilty now but when I am round there I can hear her saying things to her children that I used to say to her as a child. She changed when her dad died and I realise now that I wasn't able to think about her needs then. It was all too raw for me.*

Islay: *We can't turn back the clock and it's pointless to beat* ourselves up about the past. We do things at the time using the knowledge that we have. This links in to the Window to Self-Knowledge, when we have more knowledge or are less emotional about things we have the choice to do something different. The best thing that we can do is to stop repeating the same old patterns of behaviour.

Margaret: I've been thinking a lot about what's been prompting my behaviour and how I have been treating Damien. I've realised that as a child some of my needs were being met in very negative ways. I've realised that I wasn't to blame, I had no control over that, but it has left me feeling inadequate. I can't help what happened to me but I can do something about it now.

Paris: I have been so impressed with you, Margaret, you have been so brave and are making some great changes.

Margaret: It's really hard, as I am so used to how I normally behave, especially when Damien starts the guilt trip but I remember that you said it would often get worse before it gets better. Coming here and getting all your support has been fantastic. You have helped me believe in myself. So now if Damien thinks or says I'm crap I just think about the group, and of Paris telling me well done and I just smile. Damien says 'What are you smiling about?' in a very cross tone as it's not the reaction he's expecting.

Kim: They need to know that your love is predictable and that you are going to be consistent in what you say and the consequences you put in place. Remember a consequence needs to teach them how to behave. It's not just a punishment by itself.

Darren: I was listening to something on the radio about this. Most people think that when someone is sent to prison they will be given support and help with why they have offended and what they can do differently. If they get that type of help *then it's because they want it, it's not forced upon them. Prison is just punishment and they were saying that is probably why re-offending rates are so high.*

Islay: *If we give a punishment it is often when we are angry and full of emotion. If we tell our children we need to think about it and allow ourselves time to calm down then we are more likely to give a consequence with a reason attached to it. This means that we can teach them by giving an appropriate consequence that is fair and reasonable.*

Paris: *Riley makes me so cross that I would scream at him. I'd then tell him he was grounded for a month. After 2 days he was doing my head in so I'd tell him to go out. I'm guessing now that he knew that. I'd have been better to have just said 2 days in the first place wouldn't I?*

Martin: *The punishment needs to fit the crime as they say. I've discovered if I'm too over the top with John it makes him angry, it then makes me even angrier and in the past we would have stand up rows. I've realised that when my mum comes round and I see her being much more supportive with John than she was to me, that then makes me cross with John. It's not his fault that I've got all this history with my mum. I need to find a way to deal with that, a way that doesn't impact on my kids.*

Angie: *I once heard someone say 'The problem is not the prolem. It's their solution to the problem. So what's the problem?' That makes so much sense to me now from being on this course. I am really starting to look underneath Harry's behaviour now and I can understand him much better.*

**Give me 3 good reasons ....** Do you find yourself constantly giving reasons why your child can't have something? Next time you find yourself locked in a battle say, 'If you can come up with 3 good reasons why I should say yes. Then I'll say yes'. Your child now has to do the thinking rather than you. It is important that you do occasionally say yes to their reasons so don't only use it for things you know are completely out of the question.

It is clear that the parents have all got a lot to think about from this session. Kim asks them what they are going to focus on this week.

Margaret: *I feel really good tonight and it's made me realise that I'm doing okay. I'm going to stick with what I am doing, remember that it won't always go right and that's okay. I'm going to try to stop beating myself up and start to think about how well I'm doing.*

Martin: *I know that I have blamed everyone else for my difficulties and I feel embarrassed by my attitude. I may have contributed to John's behaviour as I wasn't taking responsibility for any of the changes. Before I was focused on all the things I couldn't change, and now through this course I have started to think differently. It's hard but I'm getting great results. Now I can change things for me and my family, it's a wonderful feeling.*

Islay: *Well done everyone, it has been a great session. It really helps if parents can step into their children's shoes and see things from their perspective. Next week's session is about conflict; during this week try to notice what your arguments are about and how you behave in an argument. Have a good week.*

As the group gets ready to leave Anne hangs back and approaches Islay for a chat.

Anne: *Islay, can I have a quick word?*

Islay: *Of course, Anne. How can I help?*

Anne: *It's about Darren; I don't think he is willing to change. It is becoming so difficult and there isn't much hope for us as a couple. That scares me.*

Islay: *I can appreciate that this is very difficult for both of you. Darren may need more time to process all of this, while you have connected with it immediately. One thing you can do is to try to separate out your feelings for him as a husband and his role as a father. His relationship with Mikki needs to be encouraged and he also needs to realise how important he is to Mikki.*

Anne: *I know that their relationship is really important but it can be so difficult as Darren insists in giving in to her and she can twist him round her little finger.*

Islay: *It is hard to manage changing relationships, especially when you feel let down and angry. When parents stop being a team often their children are able to manipulate their feelings and emotions. If you or Darren need any help during the week just give me a call.*

Anne walked away from Islay feeling glad that she had asked for help. This was becoming extremely hard work and at times it seemed like all the progress she had made was pointless. As Anne walked out of the room she was deep in thought. Islay had said people are different at processing change and it reminded her of how time had passed since she lost Roy and how her feelings had changed. Maybe there was hope for her and Darren in the future.

Darren was desperate to know what Anne had been talking to Islay about, but she didn't even mention it on the way home. Darren was struggling; there was too much going on. It was really confusing how different Anne was with him. Last night Anne had asked him whether he would go to couple counselling with her and he had been shocked. He wondered how it had got to this point. Surely counselling wasn't necessary for them – they had been so happy when they first met.

 **Do something that you love for a short time each day.** Write down the activities that you like to do, the things that are important to you, and do them.

 **FOR REFLECTION**

1. Who sets the scene in your house?

2. What need might your child be meeting in a negative way?

3. How could they meet this in a positive way?

4. What are the external influences that may be affecting your child's behaviour?

5. What are your family rules and consequences?

6. What have you learnt in this chapter that will help you to behave differently when your child is being violent?

# 9

# BRIDGE THE GAP

 **Respect each other's views.** Children will listen to their parents and respect their views, if the parents themselves respect the views of their children.

It was time for the weekly phone call to see how the parents were getting on. During the calls some of the parents shared their ongoing struggles with changing their behaviour. Paris had not made contact with Riley's dad. The man that Paris had met on the night out was her priority and Riley had been left to get on with it. Kim hoped that the phone call might encourage Paris to think about what Riley needed. On a positive note, Paris had been to the knitting group again and had really enjoyed it.

People start arriving for the session and Anne walks in alone; she confirms that Darren isn't coming to the group today. Islay asks the group how their week has been, and Anne is the first to speak,

Anne: *It's been really hard this week. I got up in the night and Darren was downstairs. I walked into the sitting room and he was sitting in the dark. I got a real fright when I put the light on. I asked him what was wrong. He said, 'nothing', but in such an angry voice that it was clear there was something wrong. I offered to make him a drink but you'd have thought I was offering him poison by the way he reacted. He went off to bed. We're hardly talking to each other so it wasn't a surprise when he said he wasn't coming tonight.*

Islay: *How has Mikki been?*

Anne: *She seems a bit oblivious to it all. Although school did call and ask if anything had happened at home. Apparently Mikki has been quite rude to her teachers.*

Angie: *That happened to Harry when Philip and I were arguing. Harry was okay at home, but he started to get really aggressive at school.*

Anne: *I hadn't thought of that. It's so hard trying to see it from everyone's point of view, when all I want to do is to curl up and cry.*

Anne starts to get upset and Angie, who she is sitting next to, puts her arm around her.

Angie: *Oh, Anne, it's hard but you are going to get through this. Whatever happens your priority needs to be with Mikki and yourself. Darren has to make his own choices. He has heard the same information as us all and ultimately he has to decide what he wants in life. Let me give you my number and we can meet up for a coffee.*

Anne (smiling at Angie): *Thank you, Angie, I'd really appreciate that. I know I have to let Darren go, if that's what he wants, but I feel so sad. He was a real support to me and I know I leaned on him a lot in the early days after Roy died. He's right it's me that's changed but he doesn't see the need to change.*

Angie: *He does still have a choice though, Anne. What about writing a letter explaining all this to him, maybe suggest couple counselling again if you feel he's too angry to talk to you.*

Anne: *Yes, I suppose I could. I need to think about whether I want this to work or whether it has gone too far now. I feel so angry.*

Kim: *It's always difficult when things change and it is so important to have support. Angie, that's really kind of you to offer to meet up with Anne. Sometimes just talking about things can help.*

Paris: *I realised after your call, Kim, that I had ignored Riley's needs and focused totally on mine. I was upset that the guy I'd met hadn't texted me. I think I have been like a statue to Riley; I was there but not really doing anything for him. I did give myself a bit of a talking to and Angie helped me talk it through at the knitting group. I contacted Riley's dad and we have arranged to meet up next week.*

Margaret: *What I have begun to realise is that I am smothering Damien. You said that you were like a statue Paris; well I have been more like an octopus with tentacles. I was stopping Damien from growing up and I was keeping him tied to me. He was probably feeling responsible for my emotions, so no wonder he was getting angry. It was his way of trying to chop off the tentacles.*

Angie: *It must be hard for you, Margaret; you have to be mum and dad to Damien so the chances are that you will be very involved with him.*

Margaret: *Thank you, Angie. Yes and last week got me thinking about how important it is to have a father-figure around, especially for boys. Damien's experience of a dad hasn't always been good; he saw his own dad beat me up. It's made me wonder what sort of man he will be when he has his own family. I'd be horrified if he ended up being like Richard. I have been trying to think who could be a good influence on Damien?*

Anne: *Have you any male relatives who could become involved?*

Margaret: *I do have an older brother. He's always saying to me 'You only have to ask if you want some help'. I suppose I could contact him, it would be hard though. He has such a perfect life and I feel like a failure.*

Islay: *That sounds like a really good idea Margaret. Ultimately it is up to us to give our children opportunities to achieve, and that will be different for each one of us. Boys need to learn how far they can go in rough and tumble games and girls need to hear positive messages to help them grow in confidence. Dads are hugely important in that. If they aren't around, for whatever reason, then you could ask for help and support to provide those messages.*

Kim: *You have shared some great insights with each other. Now, let's move on and look at how we deal with conflict. There are nine different ways of reacting to conflict. Conflict can look very different in many situations. At the root of conflict there are always two opposing views. In an argument or conflict, both people want to get their own way.*

Paris: *That sounds like me and Riley. I ask him to do something, he refuses, we end up shouting, he storms out and then I feel miserable.*

Islay: *What you are asking him to do may be reasonable, however he doesn't think so, or even if he does he doesn't want to do it, or not at the time you want him to do it. The communication level then slips down the ladder and rapport is forgotten about.*

Paris: *Yes, I just tell him how useless he is and how he never listens to me. He then gets mad and says the same to me. We end up going round in circles.*

Margaret: *How does it end?*

Paris: *In the past he has punched me. It's horrible and I get scared.*

*The last time he did it I told him I was going to call the police. I got hold of my phone but he tore it out of my hand and threw it across the room. Eventually he went out. I sat and cried. I mean how can my own son be so violent towards me?*

Martin: *My ex and I have such different ways of dealing with the children. We used to argue about it all the time.*

Kim: *Well, why wouldn't you behave differently, you are two different people who have had different experiences. As we've seen in previous sessions we will copy the important people in our lives. We will watch how they deal with conflict and unless we take time to really think about what we are doing then we will react in the same way.*

Kim: *Thinking about anger, what happens to your body when you start to feel angry?*

Margaret: *I get hot and start to shake. I can feel my heart racing. I then usually end up crying.*

Kim: *Yes, that is your body's way of trying to deal with the threat that is presenting itself. It's really important to notice anger the minute it starts to happen so that you have time to do something different.*

Martin: *I've started to do things differently. I don't lose it so much with the children. I want to try and resolve the situation for all of us.*

Islay: *It's fantastic to hear you talking in this way, Martin, and to hear about the changes you are making. To illustrate the different conflict styles we thought we'd ask you to do a bit of acting.*

There are groans and laughter in the room.

Kim: *Before we do that,though, can you give me a list of some of the things that your children do or don't do that causes arguments at home? I'm going to write it up on the flipchart.*

The parents call out in record time. They don't have to think too hard about this. Kim writes the following:

- Keeping their bedroom tidy
- Coming in late
- Not going to school
- Wearing too much make-up
- Smoking.

Kim hands out 'conflict cards' to each parent. She then asks them to get into pairs. They each look at what is written on their cards.

Islay writes the 9 conflict styles on the board.

- Blamer/Retaliator
- Storm and Tempest
- Bull in a China Shop
- Silent Seether
- Anything for a Quiet Life
- The Weeper
- Head in the Sand
- The Sulker
- Assertive.

Kim: *Using one of the examples from this list of arguments, I would like you to act out the conflict style that is written on the card. Most of you will get the chance to play both a parent and a child. Use your experience from all the arguments you have had and have some fun acting it out. On the card there are some ideas of how you might behave and what you would be likely to say in this style. Islay and I will start by having an argument about keeping the bedroom tidy. Look at what we are doing and saying and have a guess at what style we are using:*

Islay and Kim look at their cards and prepare to do battle.

Kim (child; shouting): *I ain't cleaning it and you can't make me.* (Kim gets right into Islay's face in a very threatening way.) *You can't tell me what to do. I say what happens around here not you. If I want my room like this then that's what it's going to be like* (pushes a chair over as she walks past it).

Islay (parent; weeping into a tissue and speaking softly): *How can you say that to me? I just want your bedroom a bit tidier. Why are you being so mean? I don't ask you very often. Don't be so horrible to me I can't bear it* (continues to cry).

Islay: *Okay. I'm me now! (*The group laughs.*) What style do you think Kim and I were using?*

Margaret: *Well that was me, I cry. I do that most of the time. It doesn't work as Damien doesn't seem to care. He just rolls his eyes and gets angrier. I get so upset.*

Paris: *Kim was Riley, that's what he does. He gets right up close and it looks like he's going to hit me. He will push past me. I nearly fell down the stairs the other day. I get so scared.*

Anne: *I'm guessing Islay was the Weeper, and Kim was Bull in a China Shop.*

Kim: *Yes well done, Bull in a China Shop will destroy things and has no regard for the china. In this style there is no concern for anyone else's feelings. When people use this style you often hear them say it's like a red mist takes over. Sometimes people will say afterwards that they can't remember what had happened.*

Islay: *Margaret you have described yourself as a weeper. It is a coping strategy and usually it is because the person can't cope at that point. It may be something outside of their awareness, something in Box 4. This may lead them to think, if I cry the other person will realise that I'm upset and they will stop doing the thing that is upsetting me.*

*Let's move on to Margaret and Angie for the next scene. The topic is 'coming in on time'.*

Margaret and Angie move to the center of the room, and Margaret begins:

Margaret (parent; waving a pointed finger): *I told you to come in at 9 o'clock and it is now quarter past. I knew I shouldn't have trusted you, you always let me down. You never do what I ask you to do.*

Angie (child; looking innocent): *I don't see what the problem is, what are you going on about? I said I would be in just after 9 and it is just after 9.*

Margaret (parent; moving into Angie's space): *You should've let me know you were going to be late. I told you this would happen. I won't ever trust you again. I knew I should have phoned you and reminded you. The group told me not to do it, that you had to take responsibility for yourself but how wrong were they. I knew you wouldn't remember unless I phoned you.*

Angie (child; backing away from Margaret): *You're making a big fuss about nothing, I don't know what your problem is, it's not like I'm an hour late.*

Kim: *Thank you, Margaret and Angie. Anyone like to guess which of the styles they were using?*

Martin: *Angie was Head in the Sand. I recognise that one from John. He's not bothered, whereas I'm very bothered.*

The whole group can identify with this one and they chuckle.

Anne: *Maybe it's about getting them to be bothered. At the moment all we do is stay bothered, which then makes us angry. Somehow we need to switch the care over.*

Islay: *Beautifully put, Anne. The challenge is being able to do that while staying calm. The minute it becomes more important to us that something happens then the balance has shifted. So what style was Margaret using?*

Paris: *Was that Blamer/Retaliator?*

Margaret (looking relieved that Paris had guessed right): *Phew I hate doing things like this in front of people.*

Islay: *Margaret, you did really well. You turned the blame back on yourself, which was brilliant and very common amongst parents. It links back to feeling guilty. My child is like this because I haven't been able to provide what they need. I have put them through difficult situations and so I will blame myself for it. Who else might we blame for their behaviour?*

Paris: *I've blamed the school before now. They didn't understand Riley's needs and didn't deal with him properly. I blamed his friends too, they would persuade him to do things. Well that's what he used to tell me.*

Paris realises what she has just said and has a lightbulb moment about who is responsible for Riley's behaviour.

Margaret: *I blamed Damien's dad. He saw some awful stuff that his dad put me through, but then I blamed myself for not being strong enough to stand up to him and walk away earlier.*

Islay: *Margaret what you are describing is feeling guilty which then motivates blame towards yourself. The guilt prompts your behaviour. You will have got things wrong in the past, just like all of us in this room. That's okay. None of us is perfect. It's how we make sense of it and what we then do about it.*

Kim: *So the next two who are going to have an argument for us are Martin and Anne. The topic is 'not going to school'.*

Martin and Anne look at their cards and get in the middle of the room.

Anne (child, calling out cheerfully): *I'm home.*

Martin (parent) looks upset and just grunts.

Anne: *What's wrong with you?*

Martin (speaking through gritted teeth): *Nothing why? Should there be?*

Anne: *No.*

Martin: *You sure there's nothing you want to tell me?*

Anne: *Well clearly, you think there is.*

Martin: (grinds his teeth together and rolls his eyes): *The school rang today and they have called me in for a meeting. I have had enough of this. You said you would do the timetable that they gave you last time and you haven't been anywhere near the school. Why do you say you'll do something when you have no intention of doing it?*

Anne (shrugs her shoulders, looks away): *Yeah, yeah, whatever. I'll do whatever they say.* (Under her breath) *It's all a waste of time anyway.*

Martin: *What did you say?*

Anne: *Nothing. I'll come to the meeting with you.*

Martin: *Too right you will.* He goes off and starts tutting and banging around.

Islay: *Thank you Martin and Anne. Can anyone guess which style they were using?*

Margaret: *I think Anne was a bit like me. Was it anything for a quiet life?*

Anne: *Thanks, Margaret. I'm glad that came across.*

Margaret: *It was just that you were agreeing with Martin but I could see that you didn't want to do it and I recognised that's what I do. I'm wondering if I'm a bit of a mix of the styles. I don't always want to go along with things but I tend to think people will know better than me so I'll say yes even though deep down I know I don't want to. I do it all the time with Damien. I just give in for a quiet life.*

Kim: *Do you get a quiet life Margaret?*

Margaret: *No, far from it. I wish I did.*

Paris: *Martin, were you the silent seether?*

Martin: *Yes I was. I'm impressed you got that from my bad acting.*

Paris: *It was the way you said 'nothing' that did it for me.*

Martin laughs.

Martin: *That's what my ex did all the time. I always knew there was something wrong but when I asked she'd say 'nothing'.*

Paris: *Whoops that's what I have done. It's funny, I feel upset but I don't want to talk about it I just want someone to notice that I'm upset.*

Islay: *Let's move onto the next two styles. Margaret and Paris it's your turn and the topic is 'wearing too much make-up'.*

Margaret and Paris get into place. Paris starts to stomp around.

Paris (parent, stomping around, shouting): *You are not wearing all that make-up, go and take it off immediately.*

Margaret (child, scowling, says sulkily): *What's the point in speaking to you?*

Paris (Continues to stomp around, shouting very loudly): *I am not talking about it. I am telling you take that off of your face or you're grounded for a year.*

Margaret (turns away and says under her breath): *You never listen anyway, there's no point in saying anything.*

Kim: *Thank you, that was excellent. Any ideas anyone?*

Martin: *Paris you gave us all a shock when you started shouting. I can only guess that it was Storm and Tempest.*

Paris laughing: *Yes it was and it came easily to me. That's exactly how I am at home. I think the whole street can hear me. The neighbours often bang on the walls.*

Islay: *Do you shout because you think Riley is deaf and he can't hear you?*

Paris: *No, I just can't help myself. I get so angry.*

Angie: *Was Margaret the Sulker?*

Margaret: *Yes I was. It was really easy for me too because I am a sulker. When I get upset I just go into myself and I feel so resentful. Sometimes I want to speak but the words get stuck.*

Islay: *And finally, Martin and Angie, it's your turn and the topic is 'smoking'.*

Martin and Angie position themselves in front of the group and Angie starts.

Angie (parent, giving positive attention): *I want to discuss something with you. I feel really upset because you have been seen smoking. It's important that you look after your body. I want you to stop smoking.*

Martin (child, hands on hips): *It's no big deal all my friends do it. I don't want them to leave me out.*

Angie (in a calm voice): *That must be hard for you if you feel you have to smoke to fit in.*

Martin (defensively): *Don't be so patronising, you have no idea how hard it is for me. Everyone's on my back. It's not as if you're so perfect. I've seen you having a drink.*

Angie (still staying calm): *Nevertheless I would like you to stop smoking.*

Martin (still being defensive): *You're doing my head in. I'm going out.*

Islay: *Well done to both of you. Who's going to guess?*

Margaret: *Angie was very calm and wasn't getting worked up. I think she was being assertive. She was getting her point across in a clear way.*

Angie: *Yes, thank you Margaret. I enjoyed that. It was easier doing it with Martin because I was acting. I don't always stay so calm when it's Harry – or Philip for that matter.*

Paris: *I'm guessing as we have done all the styles that Martin was doing one of the previous ones. Was it blamer/retaliator?*

Martin: *Yes it was. I realised while I was doing it how easy it is to blame someone else for what is going on. I was able to pass the responsibility, not my fault guv… It's made me think about how I've been blaming everyone else rather than looking at what I can do differently.*

Islay: *Well done everyone. It's wonderful that while doing this you've all been identifying which style you're likely to use.*

Martin: *I've just had a thought. If all these styles are about trying to get your own way, is that about being manipulative?*

Islay: Yes *it is, after all that's what conflict is all about, people wanting their own way. We all want our own way but how we go about communicating that can benefit or destroy our relationships. We need to ask ourselves: Is this important? Am I being reasonable?*

Paris: S*urely it's reasonable to expect them to clean their own bedroom?*

Kim: *Of course it is, but as a child it's not particularly high on their agenda. Conflict is normal and it would be very odd if a child never said they didn't want to do things you've asked them to do.*

Martin: *Our battles are around which TV programme they want to watch, or whether they will put their stuff away.*

Islay: *Yes that is all very normal in families and again can cause huge arguments.*

**How important is it?** In a conflict situation decide how important the issue is to you on a scale of 1 to 10. Work out how much you are prepared to give, then listen to your child and take their views into account. When the importance is put on a win-win solution both people feel valued.

Islay: *One of the things that we can begin to ask ourselves when we are getting into conflict is 'Whose problem is it?' All the time we make other people's problems our own we will feel responsible to try and change it. This is particularly important when dealing with our children. They are very happy for us to take responsibility for their problems because it means they don't have to. Their expectation will be that you will always rescue them.*

Paris: *Like taking their PE kit into school.*

Islay: *Yes, exactly like that. Sometimes when we feel powerless it seems like there is nothing we can change, we think that we will be stuck in the same situation forever.*

Kim: *We are going to look at a diagram, which may help you to work out what you can change and what you can't change.*

Kim draws this diagram on the flip chart:

| Things I can't change  X  A | Things I could change if I wanted to  X ✔  B |
|---|---|
| Things I can change  ✔  C | Where is our time spent?  A. Most of our time  B. Some of the time  C. Little time |

Islay: *The square marked 'A' holds the things that you can't change in life, can anyone say what they might be,*

Martin: *The football scores.*

Paris: *The weather.*

Angie: *School inset days.*

Everyone laughs.

Islay: *Good examples, thank you. In 'B' are the things that you could change if you wanted to, any thoughts about this one?*

Angie: *I was going to go and protest about fracking but I never got around to it.*

Anne: *I keep meaning to write to my MP about the litter in my road.*

Islay: *Great. In ' C ' are the things that you can change. What do you think they might be?*

Martin: *Asking for help?*

Paris: *Not screaming and shouting at Riley.*

Islay: *So, where would changing other people's behaviour sit?*

Paris: *In square A or is it square B?*

Martin: *It's definitely square A. We can't change anyone else only ourselves.*

Islay: *But Paris has a point, in Square B are the things we could do, and we have talked about the things you could do differently which will then force your children to change. We can't change them, only they can do that. However if we do things differently they may be forced to react in a different way. We almost have to make things so uncomfortable for them that they can't continue to behave in the same way. That's why sometimes this will sit in Square B. We could do something different if we choose to but often we will wait for someone else to do it.*

Kim: *Looking at this diagram it is good to work out where you spend most of your time and energy. If you spend it all talking about the things you have no control over then you are giving the responsibility for change to someone else. When that person doesn't change it can make us feel angry.*

Paris: *Although I'm on my own and I can make decisions for myself I know I blame other people for what is going wrong in my life. That's ridiculous isn't it? It's giving other people power over me.*

Angie: *So what you're saying is all the time I'm expecting Harry to change, it gives him power over me. It all sounds so confusing. How on earth do we get them to change then?*

Kim: *Who has tried out the 'I statement'?*

There are a few nods around the room.

Kim: *If you haven't tried it give it a go. You will find that it is a powerful way to let your child know how you want them to change. If you change what you are doing it often helps someone else to change.*

 **You have a choice.** Remind your child that they are making their own choices. When you realise that your child is choosing to behave in a certain way it will be easier for you to stay firm with the boundaries.

Kim: *We've covered a lot in this session. We've thought about conflict and how we each deal with it. You have done some great acting. (There's laughter in the group.) So before you go can you think about one thing that you could change about the way you deal with conflict?*

Paris: *Not reacting so quickly would be good for me. Another thing is every week I say I am going to make changes and then I get home and I don't bother. I've realised that I wait for your phone call each week, which reminds me that I need to do something. This week I just need to get on with it.*

Anne: *I had a lightbulb moment earlier. Watching the conflict styles I realised that instead of telling people how I feel I've been saying 'Can't you see I'm stressed?' and that's not the same at all. That must make the other person feel responsible for me. I've a feeling I've done that to the children.*

Islay: *So what could you all do differently which would mean that you are taking responsibility for the way you feel and that your children don't end up feeling responsible?*

Martin: *That's the million dollar question.*

Everyone chuckles.

Margaret: *I've realised my mood is dependent on how Damien is. That's crazy.*

Margaret is lost in thought.

Paris: *I'm the same so you've heard it here first I'm not going to do that. I feel I started when I told Riley that I wasn't rescuing him any longer. Now what I've got to do is the balance. I think I either get too involved or I am too distant. Either way it isn't very good for Riley.*

Margaret: *That sounds really good. I know I smother Damien and I need to let him take some responsibility. I need to stop being like an octopus, being so involved in his life. I have started having a bit of my own life by supporting other mums at school and by coming here. I need to continue doing that.*

Martin: *The diagram with the ABC squares meant a lot to me. I've been blaming everyone else for my problems, my children, my partners. We all end up blaming each other. I would say, 'Well if you hadn't done that then I wouldn't have done this'. It's hard admitting when you've done something wrong.*

Angie: *Yes, but none of us are perfect and we will get things wrong. In the past I have blamed work, Phillip, Harry, my parents, and myself. I realise now that this has stopped me from changing. Once I understood I could do things differently I got a feeling of power and freedom. I just knew that it was down to me. I have choices and so do others. At times that is scary but not being responsible for other people's feelings makes me feel an awful lot better.*

Paris: *Hang on a minute … what about our children? Surely we are responsible for their feelings?*

Angie: *It's an odd one this. The way I look at it is that we're not responsible for their feelings, those are their own, but we are responsible for creating relationships where they feel okay enough to share their feelings, especially when they get things wrong. If they don't feel judged they are more likely to say things like 'I've got it wrong, I shouldn't have done what I did. I've learnt by my mistake and I won't do it again'.*

Islay: *We have discussed that we can't change anyone else only ourselves. If we have to behave in a certain way to keep someone else happy then we will have internal conflict – we do it but we don't really want to. This will start as resentment and eventually build into anger.*

Angie: *I think we've all done that.*

Margaret: *That's how I was with Richard … Oh and Damien.*

Anne: *Yes, that is exactly my problem.*

Kim: *It's great that you have all recognised it. Once we know something it is impossible to not know it. That's how change happens. Your awareness has grown so that when you start to go back into familiar patterns there will be a little voice in your head that will say 'Hang on, this doesn't feel right'. It might be that you will have to stop half-way through your shouting or just before you say something. Start to listen to that voice and give yourself a chance to change. Take a deep breath and allow yourself time.*

They all look around and say almost together,

*That's it, that's what we are going to focus on this week. The inner voice telling us to stop doing what we have always done.*

They all laugh and it felt good that they would be working on the same thing during the week; there was a sense of camaraderie. The parents get up to leave and it is clear that this session has made an impact on them. As Angie picked up her handbag and made her way out of the room she thought how much she had enjoyed the role play. It was amazing how everyone in the group trusted each other now, they were so open with each other and some of the stories moved Angie to tears. Poor Anne, it was hard to imagine why Darren would jeopardize what they had built up over the last 9 years. Angie hoped they would be okay.

**Be Inspired.** Put something inspirational on your mirror. Whenever you look into your mirror you can read it and feel inspired.

## FOR REFLECTION

1. What is your conflict style? Do you have more than one style?

2. Mark yourself on a scale of 1 – 10 for the following statements.

   1 (never) and 10 (all the time):

   a) I am able to let go of the past in conflict situations.
   b) I am able to stick to the current issue in a conflict situation.

c) I choose the response I give my child in a conflict situation.

3. What could you do to improve your score?

4. What have you learned in this chapter that will help you to behave differently when your child is being violent?

# 10

# THE ENERGY BAR

**Pause and Reflect.** At the end of each day check out how you have handled things. Look at the things you have done well and think about the things that didn't go so well. How else might you have handled it?

After the previous week's session the parents had all gone away with a new enthusiasm for change. The weekly phone calls had been very encouraging. The parents had become much more aware of what was going on underneath the behaviour, both their own and their children's. Paris told Kim that surprisingly Riley's dad had turned up and after they had chatted for a while he had agreed to email Riley. Paris had told him not to expect too much from Riley and that she needed him to come back into Riley's life gradually. Anne was still finding Darren's behaviour difficult, he was behaving like a child and so far he had refused to have any proper conversation with her. Darren had adopted the typical 'sulker' conflict style and Anne was concerned that he would avoid coming back to the group.

Paris was the first to arrive, looking exhausted as she made her way to her normal seat. Kim was surprised at how deflated she seemed, and wondered what had happened. Anne arrived alone once again and as she had predicted Darren had refused to come. The group start to chat to each other and it becomes apparent that for some it had been a good week, while others had found it very challenging.

Paris: *It all started so well. I met up with Riley's dad and I didn't even need prompting with the phone call. (*The group laugh.) *He was willing to contact Riley and he sent him an email the same day. When Riley came downstairs to tell me I resisted the urge to ask Riley what his dad had said and just said 'How lovely'. I tell you it was amazing. Riley went to school, which was a miracle in itself. I had a lovely day until he came back and we argued about the TV. I wanted to watch something and he wanted to watch something else. I got really cross and all the assertive stuff went out of the window. I started moaning at him, I told him that he always spoils my fun. The next minute he slammed out of the house and didn't come back. I was so worried about him that in the end I called the police. They weren't very sympathetic and asked me what I expected them to do about it. They said they weren't his parent, I was, and he was 16. I felt miserable as I realised I could have managed the whole situation better.*

Martin: *What happened when he came back?*

Paris: *Well by then I'd managed to calm myself down. I thought about the 'blamer' style and realised that I had transferred my blame onto the police by telling them how useless they were and how they weren't helping me. I said to them 'What do you expect me to do, go and search for him on my own?' The poor guy on the end of the phone stayed really calm as I ranted. He said 'I understand how worried you must be. Can you think of something you can do rather than the things you can't do?' I was a bit shocked by that and thought, wow has he done this course?*

There are smiles in the room.

Martin: *Gosh, that must have made you remember the ABC squares.*

Paris: *Eventually it did and I thought, okay, what could I do? I decided to phone Angie after her kind offer and we talked it through. It was really helpful so thank you, Angie.*

Angie: *I didn't really do anything. You knew what you needed to do; you just needed to give yourself the space to work it out.*

Paris: *Yes, I realise that now. I got in such a state that I couldn't think straight so I went back to behaving as I normally do. Once I'd spoken to Angie I texted Riley saying I was sorry I'd yelled at him and I would like it if he came home so we could talk about it.*

Margaret: *And did he?*

Paris: *Well, he ignored me for a while and I was just about to text him again. I was starting to feel annoyed, when he texted and said he'd be back in half an hour and that he was hungry. He said to show him I was sorry I could make him breakfast.*

There's a gasp in the room.

Paris: *Don't worry I didn't fall for that one. I always have done in the past but it was different this time. Normally I would have rescued him or acted like a statue and ignored him. This time I wanted to show him I cared, but that I wasn't going to let him take advantage of me.*

Margaret: *That's what I need to do. How did you do that?*

Paris: *When he got back I offered him a breakfast bar from the cupboard. I realised he would have been hungry and remembered that was one of the things we wrote down on the iceberg that could trigger behaviour. He didn't look best pleased but he sat down and I made us both a cup of tea. While he was eating his bar* (the group laugh), *I said that I realised that there was another way I could have dealt with our argument about the TV. I tried hard not to put the blame on him and I made it clear that it wasn't fair on either of us to continue to argue. I said that I loved him and that I knew we could find a way to respect each other's likes and dislikes without it turning nasty. He got up and said 'I don't know what all the fuss is about, you should just buy me a TV of my own' and laughed. Then he said, 'Since you've started that group you've changed.' I asked him if that was in a good way or a bad way. He said, 'It's good, you seem happier'. I was stunned by that as I didn't think he'd noticed. Anyway it turned out later that he hadn't really wanted to watch a different programme. He had just said it and he didn't really know why. I know what he got out of it though; he got my attention in a bad way. I was so annoyed with myself that I'd reacted so badly. I started to beat myself up and then I heard another voice, it was yours, Kim, and you said 'Be kind to yourself, it is okay to make mistakes, that is how you learn'. I realised that I had learnt something, and that was not to react to Riley straight away. Do we ever stop learning?*

The group laugh and shake their heads. They can understand the frustration of falling back into the same old trap of behaviour patterns.

Islay: *We are going do a little exercise about how we nurture ourselves that may help you. Can you give us a list of all the things you do for yourself rather than for your child. I would like you to think about the things that you do that make you feel good.*

Kim writes the suggestions on the flipchart

## THINGS I DO TO NURTURE MYSELF

Have a bath                    Phone a friend
Go for a walk                  Meet for a coffee/pint
Read a book                    Buy a treat
Bike ride                      Date night

# THE ENERGY BAR

| | |
|---|---|
| **Swim** | **Night out** |
| **Play football** | **Yoga** |
| **Listen to music** | **Glass of wine** |
| **Have a massage-sport or aromatherapy** | **Shopping** |
| **Exercise** | **Accept help/support** |
| **Watch a film, go to the cinema** | **Get enough sleep** |

Kim and Islay are impressed with the long list but suspect that this is a wish list rather than one based in reality.

Kim: *That is a brilliant list of some great activities and hobbies which will definitely make you feel good. We have focussed deliberately on the 'doing' part of looking after yourself first. Now I would like you to think of the things that you 'say' to yourself that are kind and forgiving and then add these to the list; I'll start you off with 'I can do it'.*

## THINGS I SAY TO NURTURE MYSELF

**I can do it.**
**You will get there eventually.**
**Things have got better.**
**Well done.**
**It's okay to make a mistake.**

The parents really struggled to find positive things that they said to themselves. This was a much shorter list and Kim hoped that she could get the parents to add more to it as they went along.

Kim: *I'm going to pass around these blue glass beads and would like you to take one for each activity or saying that you do regularly to look after yourself.*

There is laughter and chat as the beads are passed around. There were quite a few beads left in the jar.

Islay: *We're going to go round the room and I want you to say one stressful situation that has happened to you this week. As you say it I would like you to put one of the beads that you are holding in this empty jar. As you put it in there tell everyone what your stress is and what positive activity the bead represents. Keep going round the group and let us know when you have lost all your beads.*

Paris started: *I got a bill through the post today that I'm going to struggle to pay.* She puts a bead down and says *I go for a night out.*

Margaret: *I ran out of cereal for breakfast today and the bread had gone mouldy.* Margaret puts down her one and only bead saying *I meet up with another mum for a coffee.*

Martin: *I forgot to buy the ingredients for Jessie's cookery lesson.* His bead represented: *I love going for a bike ride.*

Angie: *My washing machine broke down last week and my bead is going for a long walk with the dog.*

Anne: *My stress is the breakdown of my marriage* (she gets a bit tearful) *and I don't know what my bead is as I can't remember the last time I did something nice for me. I took one as I didn't want to look stupid. I used to enjoy having a long hot soak in the bath but if I go and do that now all I can hear is Mikki wailing and Darren huffing. It's awful.*

They keep going round the room talking about all the stresses that they are experiencing. There are some everyday stresses, children arguing, running out of milk, being late, getting held up by traffic, and others that need to be planned for, like birthday parties, Christmas and paying bills. Then there are the ones that take you by surprise: car or washing machine breakdown, illness or bereavement. As they pass the jar round to each other the stresses keep coming but the beads stop, apart from Paris, who seems to have a never-ending supply. Before long Paris is the only one with any beads left but for everyone there are still plenty of stresses waiting to be shared.

Angie: *Oh dear I can see what is happening. We've run out of the nice things we do for ourselves and hardly anyone has said anything kind or forgiving about themselves.*

Kim: *Yes, Angie, it seems to work something like this: as stress comes into our lives, kindness disappears, especially to ourselves. I wonder how are you all feeling?*

Together they say 'Depressed' and their body language confirms it.

Margaret: *It feels like there is a heavy feeling in the room. It seems as if all the hard work of life has landed in this one room.*

Angie: *That's it though, isn't it? Life goes on, we can't stop it and these things will happen to all of us at some point. Maybe not the breakdown of a marriage but we will all experience a breakdown of relationships. If we don't look after ourselves then it's going to be so hard to deal with everything.*

Martin: *I was thinking that you probably need a choice of a few things on your list. If you just use one thing to make you feel better then that can become too much. I was thinking when Paris said she'd have a glass of wine* (a few laugh), *it would be easy to take that to extremes and become dependent on alcohol.*

Angie: *I think that's a bit like shopping too. If I felt down I used to go and buy myself something. It never actually worked because then I'd come home and feel guilty. Especially when Philip lost his job and we had no money coming in. It became a vicious cycle.*

Islay: *So what happens when the stresses of life are overwhelming and are far greater than your ability to look after yourself in a kind, loving way? How are you going to be able to cope?*

Anne: *Probably not very well.*

Margaret: *Paris, you still have some beads left so you must be really good at looking after yourself.*

Paris: *As you say, Margaret, I am good at looking after myself, but it hasn't helped with the stresses. I still get wound up with Riley. I think he tries to be difficult sometimes when he knows I'm about to go out.*

Angie: *It's about balance again isn't it?*

Kim: *Yes. Too much of anything and it will then become a competition as our children fight to get our attention. Remember one of their fundamental needs is attention and they will get it either in a positive way or negative way. It's the opposite if we do nothing for ourselves and all our attention is on our children. It's too much for them and we will stifle them.*

Islay: *I would like you to do something for me. Can you all take a look around this room and tell me what you see that is blue?*

Martin: *The carpet.*

Angie: *Margaret's jumper.*

Islay: *Good. Now close your eyes for me and tell me the things that are in the room that are red.*

Some of the parents say, 'We weren't looking for the red'.

Anne: *I could have said my coat, because it is red and I know that, but I didn't notice anything else in the room. I was too busy looking for the blue.*

Islay: *This takes us right back to session three, where we talked about our filters and habits – can anyone remember that far back?*

Paris: *I get it. It's about what we pay attention to so the red could be the positive things in our lives, and the blue could be negative things in our lives.*

Anne: *That goes even further back in the sessions then to the very first week, when you talked about looking for our child's positive behaviour, so that could be the red that we have been unable to see.*

Islay: *Well done, yes, this exercise can be interpreted in many ways. Generally it comes down to how powerful what we're looking for is in our lives, what we are focusing on, positive or negative, becomes our reality. If what we are focusing on is negative then we will just look for the evidence to back up what we think we know. We stop looking for other evidence.*

Angie: *Is that why when Philip and I are remembering a story we both remember it differently?*

Islay: *Yes it is; you will both have focused on different aspects. Both of you are likely to be right but your attention will be on different things.*

Martin: *That's something that I have tried really hard to do, to give the kids positive attention instead of negative attention. I can spend all the time playing with them and then they'll be sitting quietly watching TV and the phone will ring and suddenly it's like all hell has broken loose.*

There is laughter in the group as they can all identify with that.

Kim: *Yes, that tells you how important you are to your children. They don't particularly want you involved with them at that moment but as soon as you are on the phone it means that they can't have you and they play up.*

Anne: *But it must be okay to be on the phone.*

Islay: *Yes of course it is. It's important that your children know you're unable to be there for them 100 per cent of the time. It's essential that they learn to be on their own and how to entertain themselves. This helps to teach them how to wait for things.*

Martin: *That's hard, especially when all they hear on the TV is that you can have it now and why wait. It's a lot of pressure.*

Angie: *I get a different type of pressure. Harry goes to a private school and the parents seem to want to try and outdo each other. It's easy to get sucked into the whole parent pressure thing. The other day I overheard a parent talking to the teacher about how they were going to buy their child the most expensive iPhone. The child is only 8. The excuse was that they felt it would help him with his homework. I think they were compensating for not giving him their time.*

Paris: *I read something on Facebook the other day. A child asked her dad how much he earned an hour at work. The child then went to her piggy bank, gave it to her dad and said, 'Here's my money can you take an hour off to spend it with me?' I nearly cried when I read that. I thought, well, at least I'm there for Riley.*

Margaret: *As you know, I don't work so I'm around for Damien, but I'm thinking that it isn't just about whether you are physically present for them but what mood you are in and how you treat them.*

Martin: *Yes, I've begun to realise that. If I'm hungry, I'm grouchy so I've started making sure I have breakfast now. I never used to; I would tell the kids 'I haven't got time because I've got to sort you lot out'. I realised I was blaming them for something that was my responsibility and not setting a good example. I've organised myself a bit better now and I get the older ones to help me in the evening to get things ready for the morning. We now all sit and have breakfast together. Thinking about it, it has made quite a difference. We are so much more relaxed than we used to be.*

**Having Fun.** Whether you are a single parent or part of a couple, find ways to have fun. Try different activities and new experiences. Invest time in your couple relationship by going on 'date nights'. Work through the alphabet: A = art gallery, B = badminton, etc.

Islay: *If you don't look after yourself then it is going to be much harder to look after your children. Equally if you spend too much time on yourself, your children will feel left out. They will then force you to pay attention to them.*

There is a general awareness that individually they have got some work to do on getting the balance right. Paris needs to think a bit less about herself and more about Riley. She does wonder whether it's too late for Riley. He is 16 after all. It was as if Martin could read her mind.

Martin: *I was wondering whether you get to a point when it's too late to change and, even if you do, maybe it's too late for your child to be affected by it.*

Angie: *I don't think it's ever too late to change. You said how much of a difference it made to you when your mum said sorry for leaving you and going out all of the time.*

Martin: *Yes you're right, it did and I was an adult then.*

Paris: *That was what I was thinking. Riley is 16 and I've realised that I've probably been quite selfish through his life. But now he needs to become independent, so it won't make any difference what I do.*

Margaret: *I think you've done really well getting Riley's dad involved and that should make a difference.*

Paris (rather subdued): *I haven't really been there for Riley. He used to come home from school and try and tell me what he'd been up to but I wasn't really interested. He obviously knew that I wasn't interested so it's no wonder he wasn't interested in school. I thought by getting mad at the school I was showing Riley I cared. I realise now that was the wrong way round.*

Kim: *Paris, I have a sense that you are giving yourself a hard time over this and I want to bring you all back to the nurturing list, particularly what we say to ourselves. I've noticed that you are all really good at supporting and encouraging each other. Islay and I have heard some terrific feedback that you have given each other. You have been treating each other like you were each other's best friends, accepting each other when things haven't gone as you had hoped. What would be lovely is if you could treat yourself like your own best friend and say these things to yourself. Give yourself credit for what you do well.*

Margaret: *It's easier to do it for someone else. I guess it's just remembering to ask, 'What would Donkey say?' again.*

Kim: *As we end the session today can you think about what you will do differently to nurture yourself this week?*

Paris: *I am going to have a go at writing things down. I already have a little notebook that I've never used. I am going to write down every time I do something for myself and then match it by doing something nice for Riley. I've a feeling it's going to be a challenge but if I can't think of doing anything nice for Riley I'll realise I've got the balance wrong.*

Martin: *I think I've realised that the nice things I do for myself are with the children. I do love it and I know I need to keep doing them but I also need to think about what I can do for myself. I used to love to play football and I belonged to a club. I think I might find out if they still meet up. I can ask my mum to babysit once a week. I also might start to think about what I could do during the day once Kyle starts school. I know it's still 18 months away, but it won't hurt to think ahead and have a plan.*

Anne: *I'm finding this really hard, as it's just so stressful at the moment at home. I like reading, so maybe I could find out about a book club.*

Angie: *Well, as you know, I love knitting and already go to the group. I've always fancied doing a quilting course at college. I'm going to see if they've got anything I could go to. I'm also going to do the writing so Paris and I can compare notes and encourage each other to keep doing it.*

As the parents wandered out of the room, Anne thought how strange it had been without Darren. On the one hand she didn't have to think too much about what she said, which was a relief, and yet she had felt lonely in the group. It made her realise how familiar it was to have Darren around; it was normal for him to be there. This made Anne think about her comfort zone, or should that be her 'familiar zone' as the last thing it seemed at the moment was comfortable. Anne was well into the stretch zone and Mikki knew it and was taking every advantage of her. Anne wondered whether her older children had been right all along. Maybe she should never have married Darren. As Anne left the room she made a mental list of her goals for the week: get some advice about the breakdown of her relationship, try to think a bit more positively, and find the time to read a book.

Martin watched Anne leave the room alone and hoped that she would think about looking after herself. Not that he was much good at it; he was struggling to ignore his old family habit, the one that said it is wrong to put your needs first. As an adult now he could understand the theory behind it, unfortunately though, it had triggered memories of the old arguments with his ex: she would want to go to the gym or meet with her friends and he would call her 'selfish'. But that was in the past now. As Islay would say, 'You can't change the past, you can only learn from it'. Martin thought about Darren and what a shame it was that Darren hadn't continued with the group; they had a laugh when they worked together in the small groups and he liked him. Darren was obviously struggling with change and the 'Is it too late for change?' thought occurred once more to Martin. Angie had come up with a good argument on the side of it's never too late when she remembered the changes his mum had made. Martin was reminded of an alternative question which was probably more relevant to Darren's situation: How many therapists does it take to change a lightbulb? Martin chuckled as he remembered the answer: Just one, but the lightbulb must want to change.

**Give support.** If you help someone else it can put things into perspective for you. If you feel trapped and isolated find a way to volunteer. Even if it is a couple of hours a week helping out at a charity shop or befriending someone who is lonely. Think about what you need and get those needs met in appropriate ways. This means that you will be better equipped to meet your children's needs in appropriate ways.

 ## FOR REFLECTION

1. How well do you nurture yourself?

2. What could you do to improve your nurturing skills?

3. What barriers do you put in the way?

4. How can you overcome them?

5. What achievements have you accomplished in your life?

6. What have you coped well with?

7. What skills do you have that will help you to manage your child's violent behaviour?

# 11

# NEW BEGINNINGS

 **Invite everyone to a family meeting.** Start by paying each other a compliment. This is an opportunity for everyone to have a say in your family life. Follow up on any actions agreed the next time you meet.

Islay and Kim talked about the changes that they had seen oto ver the course of the parenting group. The parents had become more open and honest with each other and willingly shared their feelings. Many of them had taken a huge risk to come to the group and what they had discovered was that there is no such thing as a perfect parent; they were not alone and that every parent struggles at some point. They realised that the way they managed their own feelings will have a massive impact on their children. Importantly, the parents had recognised that they were individuals as well as parents and they needed to meet their own needs as well as their child's.

To illustrate the message for this session Islay and Kim had previously informed the parents that they would not be phoning them midweek. They had reassured the parents that should a crisis occur, or if they needed to talk about anything, they could ring either of them. Paris took it hard as she liked the phone calls and found them helpful. Kim had helped her to explore what she could put in its place. Paris considered this and decided that as she was finding the knitting group helpful she could possibly get her support there. There had been no phone calls from any of the parents. Islay and Kim were interested to find out how they had got on.

All of the parents arrive at the session except for Darren. Islay and Kim observe the group as they take their seats. Everyone seems in good spirits, they watch as Martin sits down very carefully, almost as if he is in pain.

Islay: *So how did you get on with looking after yourself this week?*

Paris: *I found this quite hard. I thought that I looked after myself well, as you know I had a lot of beads last week. It wasn't until I started to write things down that I realised I was looking after myself in a negative way. The first thing I wrote was that I had bought a top, gone to the pub and had a drink and then I stopped off at a fast-food place. That was just one day. I thought about why I was doing all of this and I realised that it was mainly boredom. When I went to the knitting group, I talked to them about it. It was then that I realised all the things I do for me are about spending money. I realised things like coming here and going to the knitting group make me feel good – not buying the coolest top.*

Kim: *That sounds like you have done quite a lot of thinking this week. How was Riley?*

Paris: *Something strange happened this week and it reminded me of the last session. On Facebook people are nominating each other to think of four things to say thank you for each day for a week. My friend nominated me and it's been a real challenge. Each day I said thank you for having such a gorgeous son and I also said one nice thing he'd done. I ended up really enjoying it. I was really amazed at the reaction I got from Riley though. At first he said, 'Why have you put that rubbish on Facebook?', but I could tell he was secretly pleased, especially when my friends started to comment about it. He's even requested me to be his friend now.*

Margaret: *That is amazing, Paris, and I really like the idea of thinking of four things to be grateful for each day. I think I might get a book and do that; it might help me with losing weight.*

Angie: *Like Paris, I read something this week that made me think about being kinder to each other. It said that angry words are like banging nails into a fence. You can take the nails out, but they leave a mark, just as angry words we say can leave their mark.*

Margaret: *I met up with the mum at school and we've joined a gym. We are going along together for our introduction next week. I've been looking at my diet as well. I always thought it was more expensive to eat healthily but Damien and I went to the market after school just as it was finishing and I bought some reduced fruit and vegetables. We talked about what we could cook and people started giving us suggestions. I'm definitely going there again next week.*

Martin: *I looked into the football club and it's still going. They meet every Thursday night, so mum agreed to babysit and I went along. I found out I'm not as fit as I used to be and every bone in my body is aching. I'm definitely going back, even though I'm in pain. I'd forgotten what it was like to go out and have some fun; hopefully I will get fitter as well.*

Anne: *Well I looked for a book club and there is one not far from where I live. I rang them up and they meet on the first Wednesday of every month. I'm looking forward to going along.*

Angie: *I popped into the local community centre and they were advertising a quilting course. I couldn't believe my luck. I went along and loved it, the people were fantastic. I've paid the course fees now so I am committed to going.*

Islay: *It sounds as if you have really thought about yourselves*

*during the week, so well done. Today's session is about 'letting go',*
*which is apt as next week is the final session.*

The parents groan.

**'I'm sorry you feel that way.'** When your child says unkind and hurtful things to you instead of justifying your behaviour simply say 'I am sorry you feel that way'. When you begin to challenge your child's words in a kind way they begin to think about what they are saying.

Margaret: *I feel scared about that, as this has been a bit of a lifesaver for me.*

Islay: *Change is always hard; it means letting go of doing something and moving on to something different. It can also mean letting go of people. We'd like you to do an exercise to start this off. Can you get into pairs and talk to your partner about a situation where something had ended and you had no control or power over it. Tell your partner how you felt about it.*

Instead of moving, each parent turns to the person next to them and they soon start chatting. They are getting really good at letting each other talk and they didn't need a reminder to swap over.

Kim: *Would anyone be prepared to tell the rest of us what they talked about?*

Paris: *I talked about my Nan. I was devastated when she died. Mum threw me out when I was pregnant and Nan took me in. She always made me feel welcome and didn't judge me. She died four years ago and I still find it hard. I just think why did my Nan have to die? It's like a big empty gap in my life. My emotions get mixed up. Anger, sadness, hurt, lonely, oh I don't know.*

Margaret: *I was saying that I couldn't believe Richard left us without any warning. Although he'd been so nasty I felt like it was my fault, if I hadn't called the police on him he wouldn't have left. It made me feel stupid and I was frightened of what was going to happen to us.*

Martin: *Mine was giving up my job. It was impossible to work and look after the children. I felt let down, depressed, angry, disappointed, worried as to whether I would manage. I suffered with anxiety for a long time.*

Anne: *I feel I'm going through it at the moment because Darren is not prepared to change. I feel frustrated and annoyed with him. It's like he's letting our marriage end and there's nothing I can do about it. Even though he says he still loves me I don't see any evidence of it. I also keep thinking about what it was like when I lost Roy, the heartbreak and pain of loss.*

Angie: *This isn't about me really, but it is a time when I felt out of control. It was when Philip was made redundant. I felt the ripples of that because it affected all of us. At first I was stunned, I was worried because we had Harry in private school and we didn't know if we'd be able to afford to keep him there. We talked about selling our house and downsizing. Although it was terrifying it was also exciting. It meant things would change but it made us look at what was important in our lives. We realised that all the things we thought were important weren't important. It put things into perspective for us.*

Kim: *Thank you for sharing such difficult stories. Letting go is hard at the best of times but much harder if you have no control over it. It may present you with new possibilities, which only become clear when you look back. At the time you are likely to experience the feelings on this list:*

Kim points to the list of words that Islay has written on the flipchart. These are the feelings that the parents have experienced.

### FEELINGS (no control over an ending)

| | | |
|---|---|---|
| **Anger** | **Frightened** | **Annoyed** |
| **Sad** | **Let down** | **Stunned** |
| **Hurt** | **Depressed** | **Terrified** |
| **Lonely** | **Disappointed** | **Shook up** |
| **Worried** | **Excited** | **Anxious** |
| **Heartbroken** | **Blame** | **Frustrated** |
| **Pain** | **Stupid** | **Unloved** |

Islay: *Can you go back into the same pairs and talk about a situation that came to an end but this time it was your choice. You made the decision to let go.*

The group start chatting again and it eases the tension in the room. After 10 minutes Islay calls them back and asks if anyone would like to share what they had discussed.

Martin: *Mine was when I finally said no to my last relationship. I'd known it wasn't going to work for a while but I stayed in it. I felt relieved and a bit guilty, as she was upset.*

Angie: *When I was single, I was really unhappy at work and decided to hand in my notice even though I hadn't got another job to go to. I felt free, nervous and excited for the future. My parents were horrified as they thought I should have stayed in the job.*

Margaret: *I found this one really difficult. I realised that I haven't chosen to let go of anything. I don't normally have a say about what happens in my life, it just happens. Maybe that's why I struggle to let go of Damien.*

Anne: *I realised that my letting go is to do with Darren. He's not prepared to change so I've decided that we need to separate. The feelings are a mix of guilt, relief and sadness. My overriding feeling though is that we both need to move on and put the past behind us.*

Paris: *Like Margaret I struggled with this one as usually I am forced to let things go. When I was younger I used to smoke a lot of cannabis. About four years ago I decided to give it up. It was really hard as I used to get together with friends, have a few drinks and smoke. I stopped going out with them because I would have started again. I felt lonely at first and then really happy that I had given up. I am so glad now that I was strong enough to do it.*

Angie: *That makes me think of you, Margaret. You have chosen to lose weight and to get fitter. How does that make you feel?*

Margaret: *On a bit of a high. I feel determined and to be honest a bit powerful.*

Kim: *I love it.*

Islay: *The purpose of this exercise is to notice how different it feels when endings are forced upon you and when you decide to end something yourself. You can see the two lists. What do you notice about them?*

# NEW BEGINNINGS

**FEELINGS (some control over ending)**

| | |
|---|---|
| **Relieved** | **Moving on** |
| **Guilty** | **Lonely** |
| **Free** | **Happy** |
| **Nervous** | **Strong** |
| **Excited** | **Glad** |
| **Scared** | **High** |
| **Sadness** | **Powerful** |

Anne: *The first list has a lot of negative feelings on it. The second list, where there has been a choice, has mostly positive feelings on it.*

Kim: *Do you notice if there are any of the same feelings on both lists?*

Martin: *There is scared, excited and sadness on both of the lists.*

Kim: *Yes, with every change there is a loss and an opportunity and our feelings reflect that. Our feelings give us information about what we are experiencing, so even though they can get mixed up, here is a way of making sense of them. It links to getting our needs met which we have been talking about throughout the sessions,*

- *If our needs are met we feel HAPPY*
- *If our needs might be met we feel EXCITED*
- *If we experience loss we feel SAD*
- *If our needs might not be met we feel AFRAID*
- *If our needs are not met we feel ANGRY.*

Angie: *That is why sad is on both lists, because you will feel it regardless of whether you think the change is good or bad. I like that it is very simple and almost gives you permission to be sad. I sometimes feel I'm not allowed to be sad but I wonder if that's because it makes others feel uncomfortable.*

Margaret: *If I see that Damien is sad I immediately want to make him feel better. I think it's hard to know whether he is really feeling sad or using it to get something out of me.*

Anne: *So when we let go of our children, even though we know it is good for them we will feel sad and that is one thing that might stop us. It is painful, but natural. I am going to say that to myself then: 'It's normal and it's okay to feel sad.'*

Martin: *But if we experience these feelings I suppose our children will too, especially if they feel they have no control.*

Islay: *Yes, as we have said in the other sessions, we all need to have a sense of control in our lives. If that is taken away from us then we will have the same negative feelings. However, if you both have a sense of control then you will still get some negative feelings but the majority of the feelings will be positive.*

Margaret: *When I say to Damien 'You can't walk to school on your own', he takes it that I don't trust him and that I don't want to let him go.*

Kim: *He might also think you are trying to spoil his fun.*

Margaret: *So if I say to him, I know I need to let you walk to school but it is hard for me to let you go. How about the first few times I will follow you so I know you've got to school okay? I won't make it obvious but that way I will be able to cope. How's that?*

Kim: *Well done, Margaret, what you did there was acknowledge how hard letting go is for you. This isn't about your children. They will want you to let go of them.*

Islay: *We all carry stuff over from our childhood which motivates us without us realising it. If we allow our fear to take over then we may* never achieve our full potential. Our fear is based on the messages we have received which will tell us over and over again that we are going to fail.

Angie: *That's just reminded me of something I read somewhere. It said 'A bear paced up and down the twenty feet that was the length of his cage. When, after five years the cage was removed, the bear continued to pace up and down those twenty feet as if the cage was still there. It was for him.'*

Paris: *So what you're saying is that we stop ourselves from letting go and moving on. The past holds us back.*

Islay: *That is a lovely quote Angie, and beautifully sums up what we are saying. To be able to let go in positive ways means understanding what is holding us back.*

Margaret: *I can see that I need to let go of those messages and start to develop new ones. When I get scared of what may or may not happen to Damien I will think about the bear. Thank you, Angie.*

Martin: *Crikey Margaret, with the donkey and a bear you'll be opening your own zoo soon!*

Anne: *Ha, I can add my monkey, Mikki, in too.*

Margaret: *Let's not forget about the octopus.*

The group laugh.

Paris: *I think I've been the opposite with Riley. I've let him go too much and now he just does his own thing. He just rolls his eyes when I try to put in a consequence and ignores everything I try to do. He just does what he wants to do anyway.*

Martin: *Well that's not true because you sat him down and told him you weren't going to rescue him by lying. That was a very brave thing to do and it was letting go of him.*

Paris: *I had forgotten that, thanks for reminding me. Yes, he was a bit shocked. I have let go of the wrong things in the past and rescued him when I should have let him accept the consequences. It's all a bit of a muddle and I feel I'm only just getting the hang of this and the group is about to end. Can I come back and do it again?*

The group chuckle but we can see that Paris isn't the only one to feel like this.

Margaret: *I feel the same. I feel as if I need to hear it all over again, otherwise I won't keep it up.*

Kim: *It is always hard to let go, especially if you don't feel you are ready. Islay and I are experiencing the same with all of you, as you will feel with your children. We want you to succeed and we are fearful that you haven't had long enough to get used to using your new strategies yet.*

Angie: *I guess those are always going to be the same feelings whenever you let go of something. Are they going to survive without me? Can I trust them?*

**Allow them to make mistakes.** If you constantly rescue your child they will not learn from their mistakes. Letting your child learn through experience is teaching them to be responsible for their actions, it is part of letting them go.

Anne: *Letting go is important for our children so they can learn to take responsibility. Oh I am so slow. We've been covering this every week one way or another. I think I get it.*

Martin: *I was thinking that all through life it's a series of 'letting go's and I guess the earlier we start the better it is for our children. I know John is my oldest but I am starting to let go of him, to give him more responsibility. I've told him that I trust him but if he does anything to break that trust then there will be a consequence. He doesn't like it but I don't let him out until he lets me know where he's going, who he's going with and what time he'll be back. I think that is reasonable. I also need to know how he's getting to where he's going and how he's getting back. I tell him he has a choice and that he needs to be more responsible. It's working at the moment.*

Margaret: *I think I've just seen the light too. Letting go of our children appropriately will enable them to grow and make decisions for themselves. I think I have been trying to protect Damien against any hurt. I've wanted to protect him so he doesn't have to go through what I did. In a strange sort of a way I've done the opposite and he's not equipped now. If another child says something horrid at school to him he comes crying to me. I tell him not to be a cry-baby and to stand up for himself but I don't let him do that at home. He must be very confused.*

Paris: *I thought if I said no to Riley I was being a bad parent and he wouldn't like me. I realise now that is not how it is. Children need to hear the word no so they know what's right and wrong.*

Kim: *It also helps them to say no to others. That's really important because it keeps them safe and protected from friends who are a bad influence on them.*

Paris: *Well, I know that gets Riley into all sorts of trouble. He doesn't say no because I haven't said it to him.*

Kim: *You have all made some important points here so as we come to the end of the session can you say what you will do differently this week in respect of letting go and say also what you think the impact might be on your children.*

The group are silent. They are all thinking.

Islay: *This is probably the most difficult thing to do. Letting go is one of the hardest things you will have to do as a parent. Your worry, guilt and fear will still be there but if you can think about what your child needs rather than what you need you will be less motivated by these feelings. Maybe to help with that it would be good to turn to the person next to you. We will give out some cards and you can write on them and take them home to remind you of this session.*

Everyone looks relieved that they are going to be able to chat to the person next to them. It helps to make sense of things if you can talk it over. Kim hands out some cards and pens. The room is soon filled with chatter and Islay and Kim can hear that they are all taking this very seriously. After a while Kim asks them if they would like to share what they have written on their cards.

Martin: *I found the exercise really good. I hadn't realised how different you feel if you are in control of a decision. I need to think about that for my children. I think they have felt resentful because of my moaning and nagging. I know things have changed since I've started to take a step back. I think each time they want to pass something over to me I'm going to say to them. 'Let me think about whether I need to help you with this or whether you can try to sort this out yourself first?' It'll be interesting to see their reactions. Even with Kyle I can start to say this when he says he can't put his socks on or he can't find his boots. I'd usually huff, moan and still do it for him. But if I want him to realise that he can do things I need to start early. In the past when he has been able to find something we've lost he has been so delighted.*

Paris: *I've learnt quite a lot about myself over the last few weeks so it's hard to know what to do first. I do keep remembering that I need to be kind to myself and not beat myself up. I'm going to ask Riley to draw a picture of a fence to remind us both. I need to accept where he is and try not to change him. That means not rescuing him. He's got to go back to the police station in three weeks to answer bail and I know he's getting stressed about it. When he starts to get angry I will remember that it's probably because of that and not because of me. I'm going to keep asking myself, 'Where is this coming from?'*

Angie: *I think my Boxes 3 and 4 are getting smaller. As we have been talking I've realised that I'm quite a positive person. Even when we thought that we might have to sell our house, which was not something I would have chosen to do, I was looking at the new possibilities. Also I'm aware that I look for answers for people. I guess that could get annoying for people who don't want a solution; I can see that sometimes people just need someone to understand what they are going through. I realise that I like to help people.*

The group chuckle as Angie has been the first to share her phone number and to offer to meet and chat to people. They have all appreciated it and told her so in no uncertain terms.

Anne: *Well, I made quite a big decision earlier by saying I'm going to leave Darren. I realise that I need to give this lots of thought and it's not as simple as that. I think I've gone into extreme thinking, stay with him and put up with how things are or leave. I realise that letting go is a gradual process and Darren needs to have a say in it as well. I realise my motivation is guilt and that's also linked to my grieving for Roy. I need to let go of guilt or at least recognise when it's motivating me. I think I'm going to get good at asking myself questions of why I do what I do. I need to be aware of how my feelings of guilt relate to what I do for my children. I realise it's a slow process but I do feel I am beginning to have a better understanding of myself.*

Margaret: *Well … apart from starting a zoo …*

Everyone laughs.

Margaret: *Seriously though this has given me such a lot to think about. I was made to feel over-responsible as a child and I have now done that to Damien without realising it. I'm going to ring my brother and ask him for some support. I know Damien loves me and no one will take my place but I also know that Damien needs other people in his life.*

As the group prepare to leave there are murmurs about the final session next week. Some of the parents have taken responsibility for continuing the support group. Paris has already made a closed group on Facebook where they are able to talk to each other privately and not wanting to leave anyone out; she has offered to give lessons to those who are not Facebook users.

Paris waited for Margaret and they walked out together. Paris was struck by how Margaret looked now compared to when she had first met her. In the early days Margaret didn't really look at her, whenever anyone spoke to her she kept her eyes fixed on the floor. Paris had found a kindred spirit in Margaret; she had been through hard times just like she had, she was strong and never gave up. She reminded Paris of her Nan. It had been hard not to cry today, her feelings had taken her by surprise and it showed how much she missed Nan. Paris realised that no one had filled that gap in her life; it was a huge gap to fill. Today she'd learnt lots of things but the main one was that it wasn't Riley's job to make it better; that was something that she needed to do. Paris wondered what the future held for her as she started to chat to Margaret. Margaret had a lot to do this week: ring her brother, go to the market, to a gym induction, and it was tiring just thinking about it. But she had never been happier, she had a purpose, and that was to get fit and be healthy. Margaret understood now, if she wanted Damien to do things differently she had to show him how. As they left the building Paris said 'I'm not looking forward to the last session are you Margaret?' and Margaret replied 'I'm dreading it'.

---

 **Appreciate who you are.** Listen to what you say to yourself, and how you talk about yourself. Start to appreciate your strengths and abilities and build upon them.

---

 **FOR REFLECTION**

1. What was your experience of being let go of by your parents?

2. Do you think that your parents let go of you in a healthy way?

3. Do you manage feelings of loss? Do they overwhelm you?

4. What behaviour do you use to avoid letting go? Is it:
   a) Conflict
   b) Denying feelings
   c) Rescuing
   d) Something else

5. What would help you to let go in a healthy way?

6. What have you learned about letting go that will help you to manage your child's violent behaviour?

# 12

# A WONDERFUL VIEW

 **Actions speak louder than words.** Children are sensitive to what parents say and what they do. If your words and actions match up your child will have confidence in you.

As the final session approached, Islay and Kim waited to see whether any of the parents would phone them. There had been no phone calls received, however Kim had made the decision to ring Darren and offer him support. When she spoke to him he was fairly non-committal, he sounded lost and confused about the situation. He told Kim that Martin had rung him and invited him to meet up at the pub that evening. Kim encouraged Darren to come back to the last session; she said that it would be lovely to see him there. He told her that he would think about it but he probably wouldn't come. He went on to say that it had become very difficult between him and Anne and he didn't want to spoil it for everyone in the group. Kim ended the call by saying that she hoped he had a good time that night with Martin.

The group return and once again Anne arrives alone. Margaret is late and everyone is concerned that she won't make it at all. When she arrives she looks quite sad. She apologises to everyone as she hurriedly sits in her seat.

Angie had contacted everyone and suggested that they all bring snacks to share. It gave the impression of a party.

Angie: *I thought that as it was our last session we needed to mark the occasion. We all decided to bring a few snacks along with us.*

Islay: *It's lovely, thank you. Shall we eat and chat or do you want to leave it till a bit later?*

Margaret: *Can we leave it until later or otherwise I think I will be distracted.*

The group agree to Margaret's suggestion. Paris comments on how Margaret had really moved up the communication triangle. She praised Margaret for speaking out so confidently and reminded her that this wouldn't have happened a while ago.

Margaret: *I know. I do feel more confident but I really struggled with coming tonight. I think it was the saying goodbye. I wanted to stay at home, like I would have done in the past. I knew that this time though I needed to come.*

Angie: *Oh, Margaret, you've done so well and I am quite sure that this isn't going to be the last time we see each other. I know it will change and we won't be coming here every week, but there is always a time to let go, like we discussed last week. It will be okay because we will be keeping in touch with each other; especially now we've got the closed group on Facebook.*

Margaret smiles: *Yes I know and that's what I said to myself. Damien insisted I should come and that I would only feel sad if I didn't. Anyway he said I had to come as I was bringing the crisps, he said you couldn't have dip without crisps.*

Paris: *Well good for Damien, because we would have really missed you if you hadn't come.*

The group smile their agreement.

Paris: *I'd like to start, if that's okay with everyone?* They nod their heads.

Paris: *I asked Riley to draw the fence and I've brought it for you all to see. He's done so well.*

She shows everyone Riley's drawing, which clearly shows some holes in the fence. There's one hole with the nail half in and some with the nails still in. It's a beautiful drawing.

Paris: *He grumbled a bit but sat down and drew it straight away. It seemed to catch his imagination. This week if I have been about to say nasty things to Riley I've made a point of looking at the fence and asking myself which hole I am focusing on. Keeping the nail in or pushing it out? It has really worked and it has stopped me from having a go and getting sucked in. I have kept my writing up and I have started to do nice things for Riley. The other day when I was out shopping I saw his favourite cake and I bought it for him. When he came back from school I could see he was in a bit of a mood. Normally I'd have had a go at him but I did something different. I showed him the cake and said when I'd seen it I'd thought of him. I said, 'I know you love these so I bought it for you'. I could see it meant such a lot to him that I had been thinking of him when he was at school. It made me realise that this was probably the first time I'd ever done anything like that. It was when you said, Martin, that it was never too late to be there for him. Things have been better this week. I know I've got a long way to go but I also know that as long as I keep asking myself 'What message am I giving?' then I will be able to cope.*

Martin: *You are an inspiration, Paris. I like the idea of doing something nice. I have started to notice when the children are doing something right and I'm letting them know. I've realised that it is a fine balance – there's that word again – between noticing and telling them when they have done something right and going over the top and constantly praising them. I read something about this. It said that if you keep praising them then they'll expect it all the time and get disappointed for just doing something that is expected of them. It can cause them problems when they go to work. They expect to be praised all the time. I've started saying, 'Thank you, that's what I expected you to do'. It seems to be working. Each of the children has a day when it is their turn to choose what we all have for dinner. The other day it was Jessie's turn to choose the meal and she had noticed that Lucy was a bit down, so she said, 'Lucy I would like you to have my turn today'. Lucy was so happy. I made a point of praising Jessie for being so thoughtful.*

**The rule is ...** Make sure that your rules are in place and everyone knows what they are. If you find yourself getting sucked into an argument say clearly and confidently 'The rule is ...'.

Margaret: *I hadn't thought of the different ways we praise them but that seems to make sense. When Damien does something I ask him to do, I'm so grateful that I go a bit over the top. I wonder what he thinks.*

Martin: *He probably thinks that he only has to do something small to make you happy and then he can go back to behaving how he normally does.*

Paris: *I know what you mean, Margaret. If Riley comes in on time then I am so relieved, but really he should come in when I ask him* to. He can be horrible to me and say some really hurtful things. In the past when he was nasty to me and I'd almost lost it with him he would make me a cup of tea. Me, being a softy, would be so grateful that he had done it I would praise him up. I realise it was far too much. When he tells me to get lost and that I'm useless I now say, 'I'm sorry you feel like that'. It makes him stop. I've stopped trying to justify myself to him. It makes him realise what he is saying. I know he doesn't mean it because he has started to come back later and say sorry. I just say thank you for saying sorry.

Martin: I'm the same; I'm not getting caught up in all their dramas so much. After last week I decided to call a family meeting. I said that I felt they were all capable of having some responsibility and we were going to decide what that would be. I'd made up a list of things I expected them to do and told them that they could earn some money if they did extra jobs on top of their expected ones. They all really liked the idea. We wrote up who was going to do what jobs and what the extra ones were. John has actually cleaned the car for me this week. That was an extra job. The expected jobs are simple things like making their beds, putting their dirty washing in the wash basket. All things that they need to learn to do for themselves. I also met Darren at the pub and he says hello.

There are murmurs of 'How is he?' 'That was a nice thing to do' round the room. Anne also looks pleased that they had met up.

Martin: It was good. We chatted and had a laugh. I felt quite sad when he stopped coming. We're going to meet up regularly. I hope you don't mind, Anne?

Anne: No, not at all. In fact I could tell that Darren was happy when he got back. I think he had felt left out. I can understand why he didn't want to come back here with the difficulties we are having, but he really does need someone to talk to.

Margaret: *How are things at home for you, Anne?*

Anne: *Last week had quite an impact on me. Coming here has really opened my eyes. I feel as if I've woken up. I know it sounds strange but I think I have been going through the motions of life rather than really living it. I've started to think more about why I do what I do and whether I still need to keep doing it. I went to see Sophie. I explained that I love her and want to help her as much as possible. I said I might not be able to help out as much as I have been, because of what is going on and I didn't want to let her down. I said I wondered if we could have a set time when I would visit her or when they would come to me. That way she'll be able to plan ahead and do the things that she finds hard with the children in tow. She was a bit put out to begin with, but we got chatting about her dad. It was the first time we'd done that and somehow I think something has shifted in our relationship. I realise that I try to protect her and I've never given her the opportunity to grow up. I've stopped seeing her as this helpless person and I have started to see her as the capable person she is. At the moment things are okay. The test will come when she rings me at the last minute and expects me to drop everything. That's when it is going to be hard to do something different.*

Margaret: *I've had a thought. When she does ring, instead of rescuing her, you could say, 'That must be really difficult for you.' Then you are acknowledging her feelings. She is likely to say, 'Yes, it is', as she'll still be expecting you to say you'll help out. Then you say 'What do you think you can do about it?'*

Anne starts laughing.

Anne: *That is a brilliant idea. Then she'll have to come up with her own solution. When she rings me it is all doom and gloom and I do get sucked in, I'm still trying to make it better for her. That is an excellent suggestion as it will stop me saying I'll sort it out and it will help Sophie to think things through. I love it, thank you so much.*

Martin: *I'm going to use that on the kids as well. I like that one.*

Margaret: *Ah, I'm really glad you like the idea. It was when we were talking about giving our children responsibility and how that helps them grow that made me think of it. I like watching wildlife programmes and one I watched was about cheetahs. They said that for cubs to survive, the lessons learned in early life are the foundation for later on. I realise that we need to give our children good foundations and then keep them on track by getting them to think for themselves. I did that to Damien yesterday when he came home from school. He was moaning about one of the teachers and I said, 'That must be difficult for you?' followed by 'What do you think you can do about it?' It got him thinking and I could see he was really proud of himself when he came up with a good suggestion. I know we talked about it earlier in one of the sessions but I'm not sure it meant so much to me. It's had such an impact now though.*

Paris: *I've been longing to ask, did you ring your brother?*

Margaret: *Yes, I did and he sounded really pleased I'd rung him. We met up for a coffee and he was really sweet. I explained that I was finding it hard to let Damien go and how I realised that I needed to for his sake. He was great; he listened and was very supportive. He came round after Damien had finished school in the week. He just sat and chatted with Damien and they played a game together. We agreed that it would be best to start it like that and he's going to come round once a week. It was so nice and he stayed for tea. Damien seemed to enjoy it. He gave me a great tip too, I tried it with Damien and it worked. He said to me that when Damien doesn't do what I ask, instead of getting sucked into an argument, it was a good time to become like a broken record.*

Paris looks confused: *What's one of them?*

People start to laugh and then realise that she truly may not know what a record is.

Martin: *Well Paris, in the olden days* (people are still laughing) *to listen to music you had a record and a record player.*

Paris (sarcastically): *Yes – I have seen one of those.*

Martin: *Sometimes the record would get stuck in a groove and you would hear the same word over and over again until you went and moved it on.*

Paris: *Oh, no, I hadn't realised that. I'm beginning to see what you are saying; it's when you tell someone the same message over and over again.*

Margaret: *Yes that's it. My brother said instead of giving different reasons why he can't do something, I need to say the same thing over and over again. When Damien wanted his friends to come in late one evening last week we started to get into a shouting match. I stopped and remembered the broken record. When he kept on about them coming in I said, 'I know that you want them to come in, but nevertheless it is too late and they can come back tomorrow.' Damien carried on trying to change my mind. The only thing I changed was the first word, sometimes I said 'Regardless' instead of 'Nevertheless'. Eventually he said 'You're unfair. I hate you'. I said, 'I'm sorry you feel like that.' He stomped off and went to his room. I was really chuffed that I'd stayed strong, and that they didn't come in. I am going to keep doing it, because it works. It's brilliant.*

Angie: *That reminds me of one of my aunts who died a few years ago. She had dementia and when I visited her she would ask me about the family. I would go through everyone and she would nod* and then ask me the same question. 'How's the family?' I would then think of different things to say but would soon run out of ways of saying the same thing. In the end I would just repeat the same thing, like a broken record. She didn't know it was happening and it was easier for me. We would have the same conversation several times over until it was time for me to go. She was happy and that was what counted. I am going to try that with Harry, I am sure it would work with him. I like the idea of writing the rules down too. Everyone is clear about what is expected. Harry is very good at convincing me I didn't ask him to do something. He is so good at it that I start to doubt myself.

Paris: *That's like Riley. Sadly, I can't believe anything he tells me.*

Martin: *My counsellor said an interesting thing to me once. He said when something is bothering you ask yourself, 'Is this going to be a problem for me in 5 years time?' It's definitely helped me to put things into perspective. With John it has helped me to think differently about the problems at school and I don't get so sucked in. I look at him and say, 'I'd love to help but there are some things that you need to learn to do for yourself. If I do them for you then I won't be doing you any favours. I am here though, if you want to talk things over with me.' Like you've all been saying it's about handing the responsibility over to them rather than taking it for them.*

Angie: *I've had a good week. Last week made me question my motivation for wanting to help people. It's been good for me. I've also realised that my need to help others has impacted on Harry. I've often dragged him to people's houses after school, which I know he hates. He just wants to get home to do his thing. I've decided that if I offer help it's going to be when Harry is at school. He made a comment yesterday about how nice it's been just being the two of us after school. It hit me then how he must have felt left out and that other people were more important than him. There was* one idea I thought I must share with you as I found it really funny how well it worked. I am on the parents' association at school and we had a meeting. Well you can imagine how the parents all want their ideas to be listened to and it became a bit of a shambles and no one was listening. They were all trying to out do each other. The Chair eventually banged on the table and said, 'Enough!' in a very loud voice. Everyone instantly went quiet. She then went on to say that we couldn't hear what anyone was saying. She had a pen in her hand and she said that from now on you could only talk if you were holding the pen and we would pass it around. You had to wait your turn. You weren't allowed to comment on anyone else's suggestion, only to give yours. If you didn't have anything to say that was fine you could just pass the pen onto the next person. The pen was passed around and all the suggestions were written up on the board. It was hilarious watching some of the parents as they found it so hard not to talk. It worked incredibly well. In fact one of the mums is very shy and doesn't say anything. Well, when it was her turn with the pen, she was very nervous but put forward this amazing suggestion. You could see that everyone in the room was really impressed and in the end that was the one everyone voted for. She had the biggest smile on her face. I thought using a pen was a brilliant idea and how we would have missed out on a very good idea if the Chair hadn't suggested it. I was thinking that would transfer really well to families where everyone wants to have their say and no one wants to listen to anyone else.

Martin: *That is such an excellent idea. I am definitely going to use it at our next family meeting and I think it should be called the Listening Pen because it makes people listen to each other. That's genius.*

Angie: *I think I'm going to buy a special pen and put it on the mantlepiece. I think I'll pick it up and tell Phillip and Harry I've got something important to tell them and when I've got their attention I'll tell them I love them.*

The group smile as they like that idea.

**Team work.** Children are very good at divide and separate. When there are decisions to be made regarding your child make sure that you include all of the people who are important in your child's life. It might mean putting aside your differences and finding a way to communicate with an ex-partner.

Islay: *You have all done so well. Today we have heard how you are taking what you have learnt in the group and using it at home with some good results. When you first came to the group it seemed like you had no solution to your problems and now even though there are still problems you are all finding some fantastic solutions.*

Islay turns to Kim and says '*Our work here is done*'.

The group laugh, but you can see that they agree. The change has happened. When we first met them they had been stuck with no way out, and they were repeating patterns of behaviour that didn't work for them. Now they were recognising that although they will always have problems to deal with, they have the knowledge and confidence to do something different. Doing something different will give them the different outcome they desire. As the group comes to an end there is a feeling of peace and pleasure as the parents share the food and arrange to keep in touch.

**Finally ... and always:** Look at the things you've done well and celebrate your success.

We are all on a journey in our lives. It is up to us to determine where we will go and who will join us on this journey. Be clear about your journey. Work out what you want in life. If it is a happy home life without violence then look at what you can change. Check who is in the driving seat of your life and if it isn't you then who is it? Are you happy for them to be there? Do you need to take over? Remember, it is up to you. Enjoy life; it is only as hard as you make it. Yes, the pressures are there and they will stay there. But like the parents in the group you can find the solutions rather than getting stuck. Throughout their journey the parents have shown us that there are solutions to be found if you pick up the mirror rather than the magnifying glass. Be brave. Pick up the mirror and find the laughter in your soul. It is there. It is there within everyone.

If you have made positive changes in your lives, like the parents in this book, please visit our our website: www.mvchild.info and let us know what has worked for you.

# EPILOGUE

These are the practical tools that will help a parent deal with most situations. These are power tools which when used regularly can transform and improve relationships. Their value is that they strengthen the skills, which are required to be an assertive parent: warmth, empathy and understanding alongside clear boundaries and consequences. The tools have been divided into de-escalating tools and maintenance tools. The de-escalating tools will be invaluable when you have a crisis on your hands or if you find yourself frequently in a war zone at home. The maintenance tools can be used to repair and build positive relationships and are also a preventative measure against relationship breakdown. The following tools have been described throughout the sessions in the book. The number in the bracket ( ) relates to the number of the tool in the chart.

## Tools for De-escalating

| 1 Collect information | 2 Give me 3 good reasons | 3 Walk away | 4 Stay calm |
|---|---|---|---|
| 5 Say 'Regardless' or 'Nevertheless' | 6 I Statement | 7 Less shouting | 8 The Listening Pen |
| 9 Team work | 10 Sorry you feel that way | 11 Broken Record | 12 It is important to ... |
| 13 The rule is ... | 14 Negotiate | 15 You have a choice | 16 Listen for feelings |

## De-escalating Tools

These tools will help you to set boundaries in a loving way supported by all the adults in your child's life (9). Being explicit with the rules, including giving reminders (13), and being clear about your expectations (12) gives your child the choice to conform (15). This helps you to keep your boundaries firm. Your child may resist the rules and boundaries that have been set in place. Good communication skills, including 'I' messages (6), phrases such as 'regardless' or 'nevertheless' (5) and assertiveness techniques (11) will help you stay on track. The most effective way to manage conflict is to stay calm (4). We need to stay calm so that we can listen for feelings (16) and collect information (1). One way to stay calm is to stop shouting (7) and take time out if required (3). Working towards a win-win situation (14) is a positive resolution to conflict. A phrase that can be used to diffuse conflict is 'I'm sorry you feel that way' (10). Allow your child to persuade you by asking 'Give me 3 good reasons why I should say yes' (2). When communication is breaking down between you one way of enabling both you and your child to be heard is the listening pen (8).

## Tools for Maintenance

| 17 Clear boundaries | 18 One-to-one time | 19 Small gifts and gestures | 20 Three things in common |
|---|---|---|---|
| 21 More praise | 22 Allow them to make mistakes | 23 Age appropriate consequences | 24 Look for the positive |
| 25 Give responsibility | 26 Ask for their opinion | 27 Family meeting | 28 Set an example |
| 29 Ask questions | 30 Say sorry | 31 Have fun together | 32 Say thank you |

## Maintenance Tools

Maintain your relationship with your child by treating them with love, respect and kindness. Show your child that you love them by dedicating some of your time to them (18). Find out what you have in common (20) and make the time to have fun together (31). Your child wants your approval and needs your attention so look for the positive (24) and give feedback to encourage your child (21). Let your child know that you respect them by asking for their opinion (26). Show that you are interested in their life by asking questions (29) and that you like them by treating them with kindness, generosity (19) and appreciation (32). Setting firm boundaries in a loving way will provide a consistent approach (17). Give your child age-appropriate consequences (23) and allow them to make mistakes (22); this will help them become responsible for their own actions. Give your child responsibility (25) and allow them to have a voice within the family (27) so that they can learn to be independent. An essential part of maintaining relationships is the willingness to repair any damage. Saying sorry (30) for your actions is a positive example to your child (28).

# ACKNOWLEDGEMENTS

To Amy Michelle Downey, with many thanks for your commitment and inspiration which made the illustrations come to life.

To David Ashe for your amazing ideas and suggestions, which enhanced this book, we are very grateful.

To DLT who put their faith and trust in us to make our vision a reality. In particular to David Moloney whose patience and tact helped us enormously during the creative process. Also our thanks to Helen Porter for her help and guidance along the way.

To our family and friends who have encouraged and supported us on this journey with patience and understanding.

Last but not least, our thanks to each other for making this book happen. We both acknowledge that this book was formed in the knowledge, dedication, and laughter that our friendship provides.